KV-680-830

Business Objects Companion

David Jackson

Prentice Hall PTR
Upper Saddle River, NJ 07458
www.phptr.com

ISBN 0-13-977406-8

9 780139 774065

90000

Library of Congress Cataloging-in-Publication Data

Jackson, David, 1948-
  Business objects companion / by David Jackson.
     p.   cm.
  Includes index.
  ISBN 0-13-977406-8
  1. Relational databases. 2. Business Objects. 3. Business--Data
processing. I. Title
QA76.9.D3J317 1998
651.8'57565--dc21   98-4208
                                                     CIP

Editorial/Production Supervision: *Maria Molinari*
Acquisitions Editor: *Jeffrey Pepper*
Manufacturing Manager: *Alexis R. Heydt*
Cover Design Direction: *Jerry Votta*
Cover Design: *Anthony Gemmellaro*
Marketing Manager: *Miles Williams*
Compositor/Production Services: *Courier Westford, Inc.*

© 1998 Prentice Hall PTR
Prentice-Hall, Inc.
A Simon & Schuster Company
Upper Saddle River, NJ 07458

Prentice Hall books are widely used by corporations and government agencies for training, marketing, and resale. The publisher offers discounts on this book when ordered in bulk quantities.

For more information, contact
        Corporate Sales Department,
        Phone: 800-382-3419; FAX: 201-236-7141
        E-mail (Internet): corpsales@prenhall.com
Or write: Prentice Hall PTR
        Corp. Sales Department
        One Lake Street
        Upper Saddle River, NJ 07458

All rights reserved. No part of this book may be reproduced, in any form or by any means, without permission in writing from the publisher.

Printed in the United States of America

10 9 8 7 6 5 4 3 2 1

ISBN 0-13-977406-8

Prentice-Hall International (UK) Limited, *London*
Prentice-Hall of Australia Pty. Limited, *Sydney*
Prentice-Hall Canada Inc., *Toronto*
Prentice-Hall Hispanoamericana, S.A., *Mexico*
Prentice-Hall of India Private Limited, *New Delhi*
Prentice-Hall of Japan, Inc., *Tokyo*
Simon & Schuster Asia Pte. Ltd., *Singapore*
Editora Prentice-Hall do Brasil, Ltda., *Rio de Janeiro*

All information is imperfect. It has to be treated with humility.

Dr Jacob Bronowski

To
Andrea and Peter

Acknowledgements

Gratitude is due to Charles Nicholls, Business Objects' UK Marketing Director,
for his support and provision of materials.

Table of Contents

Table of Contents

CHAPTER 1

Introduction

U nderlying virtually every modern computerized information system is a relational database. The traditional way in which business end users - accountants, engineers and managers - are able to view the contents of their databases is by looking at the screens and printed reports provided for them by people whose business is computing. And on the face of it, this is sensible because it shields those business users from having to gain experience in the art of relational data modeling, in the use of programming languages (particularly SQL) and in the variety of software tools needed for building the screens and reports; not to mention having to take the time and trouble to study the internal structure of their own databases, once they have gained the expertise necessary to do it.

However, given the infinite number of ways in which the information contained within a given database can be selected, ordered, summarized, aggregated, tabulated and charted, end users inevitably suffer the never ending trickle of expenditure of time and cost as more and more reports and query screens are requested from computer departments.

The *Business Objects* software product provides the solution to the conundrum of, on the one hand, the business user who has neither the time nor inclination to become a computer expert and on the other, the never ending need to call upon the computer department to build yet another reporting program.

Business Objects provides a tool set which enables computer professionals to build user-friendly *interfaces* between relational database and business end user, enabling the content and structure of the database to become understandable and accessible. Another *Business Objects* tool set enables business end users to freely and selectively extract information from their databases, as viewed through the interface, and copy it into their own PCs for further analysis and manipulation.

A comprehensive set of further end user tools enable the extracted information to be analyzed on the end user's PC in a variety of ways and the results formatted into reports and charts. These tools are powerful and include drill-down and data mining facilities.

There are essentially three types of Business Objects users:
>   Designer
>   End user
>   Supervisor

Designers create the special interfaces referred to above (described in Business Objects' terms as *Universes*) through which end users are able to visualize and extract information from their databases. There will normally be a single Designer within any Business Objects community. Each Designer will have a PC on which the Business Objects *Designer* software module will have been installed and which PC will be remotely linked to the server database on which the end user's business information is stored.

There will be several end users and each will have a PC which will be remotely linked to the server database and on which the Business Objects end user software module will have been installed. End users could be sub divided into *experts* and *novices*. The latter are much the same as traditional end users and will make requests of expert end users, or the Designer, to create ready-written database queries and reports on their behalf. Expert end users will create database queries and format the results into reports and charts.

The *Supervisor* will provide end users with access to the various Universes created by the Designer. This is achieved by creating a special administrative database on a remote server, referred to in Business Objects terms as a *Repository*, to which all end users' PCs will be linked. This database will hold information about end users and Universes, and a matrix in which the former are given access rights to the latter.

The Supervisor's PC is thus one on which the Business Objects *Supervisor* software module has been installed and networked to both the business information database and the Repository database, which may or may not be sharing the same server platform.

This book aims to provide a narrative based description of the Business Objects product and can be used in conjunction with the manuals supplied with the product and the contextual help facilities available online.

Chapter 2 provides an overview of relational data modeling, aimed at those already familiar with the subject, and intended to introduce some of the concepts relevant to the use of the Business Objects product.

Chapter 3 continues on the subject of data modeling with particular emphasis on the best way to structure data for use with Business Objects.

Chapter 4 describes the Business Objects *Designer* software module and how it is used to construct a friendly interface between the data model and end user.

Chapters 5 through 8 describe a range of Business Objects end user tools which can be used for analyzing and reporting on PC-based data that has been extracted from the database via the interface.

Chapter 9 describes how users, and their accessibility to Universes and software modules, are administered centrally.

Chapter 10 describes how Business Objects can be integrated with the Microsoft Excel spreadsheet products enabling database queries to be triggered from within Excel sessions and the results inserted directly into worksheet cells.

CHAPTER 2

Overview of Relational Data Modeling

T here follows an overview of relational data modeling aimed at those already familiar with the subject and intending to introduce some of the concepts relevant to the use of the Business Objects product.

A relational database is a structured collection of data files, or *tables*, held on permanent media such as magnetic disks. Each table is associated with a particular category of information and will contain records representing instances of that category. Records are collections of data items (or *attributes*) and all the records of a particular table will have the same number and structure of data items - only their values varying from record to record. A table's records and attributes are more popularly described as *rows* and *columns* respectively.

One or more of a table's attributes will take values that uniquely identify the table's records and these attributes are referred to as the table's *primary key(s)*.

Information is extracted from database tables using the standard query language SQL which, in its simplest form, is structured as shown below:

```
select     (list of attribute names)
from       (table name)
where      (record selection criteria)
```

The result of any piece of SQL is a subset of the table's rows and columns. The SQL simply reduces the number of rows (according to the record selection criteria in the *where* clause) and the number of columns (according to the *select* clause items) of the table (in the *from* clause).

A database table will usually be related to one or more of the database's other tables in a *parent-child* relationship in which one record of the parent table will have a number of the child table's records related to it. For example, a record in a table of *counties* will have associated with it a number of records in a table of *towns*. A table can have more than one child table associated with it and might itself be a child table of several parent tables. A parent-child relationship is maintained simply by reserving one of the attributes of the records in the child table (towns) for the primary key value of the associated record in the parent table (counties).

Some *parent* tables merely serve as code translators, enabling codes in child tables to be translated into full descriptions. Such tables are usually referred to as *reference* or *look-up* tables.

2.1 Aggregating and Removing Duplicate Records.

The number of rows resulting from a piece of SQL can be further reduced, irrespective of any *where* criteria, in two ways:

- Placing the *distinct* qualifier after the *select* keyword will remove all but one of any set of duplicated result lines (i.e. result lines with identical values throughout).

- Using one of the available *group functions* (sum(), max(), avg() etc) in conjunction with the *group by* clause.

For example, both the following pieces of SQL will produce one result line for each distinct nationality (the second SQL statement also produces associated population counts).

```
select distinct nationality          select nationality,count(surname)
from employees                        from employees
                                      group by nationality
```

2.2 Joins

The parent and child tables, described earlier, can be combined (or *joined*) within the same piece of SQL. In such cases, the *where* clause will need to include, in addition to any record selection criteria, the *matching criteria* needed for the join.

For joined tables, the SQL will take the following general form:

```
select      (list of attribute names)
from        (list of table names)
where       (record selection criteria)
and         (matching criteria)
```

The matching criteria is essentially a list of statements of the form

```
parent-table-name.column_name = child-table-name.column_name
```

(one for each component (attribute) of the parent table's primary key)

The rows resulting from the joining of two tables are those which satisfy both matching criteria and record selection criteria.

Joined tables are generally depicted as shown below left, or more usually as shown below right, where not all parent tables have children.

The join can, however, be widened to include the non matching rows of either (but not both) of a pair of joined tables through the use of an *outer join*. An outer join is normally specified in the SQL by the placing of the + sign in each of, and at one side of, the matching criteria statements associated with the joined table pair.

e.g.   `parent-table-name.column_name = child-table name.column_name(+)`

A special join is where a table record is joined to another of its own records. This relationship is commonly referred to as the *pig's ear* and can be used to represent hierarchical trees.

2.3 Group Functions

Group functions should be handled with care. Specifically, the *sum()* function's values should never include attributes of a parent table. This is because parent table attributes will always be repeated for each associated child record in any results set and any *sum()* function will not ignore repeating values. The same goes for the *count()* and *avg()* functions, although count(distinct ..) can be used safely on parent tables, as can the *min()* and *max()* functions.

Note, however, that summed parent-table values are safe if used as denominators or products of summed child-table value ratios.

i.e. both the following are valid:

```
sum(child-table column value/parent-table column value)
sum(child-table column value * parent-table column value)
```

However, where both column values are from a child-table, they must be treated as follows:

```
sum(child-table column value)/sum(child-table column value)
sum(child-table column value)*sum(child-table column value)
```

These dangers associated with the use of group functions are important and will be mentioned again in Chapter 3.

2.4 Aliases

It is occasionally necessary to join a parent table to more than one of the tables involved in a piece of SQL. An example is illustrated below in which the nationality of both salesman and customer are required.

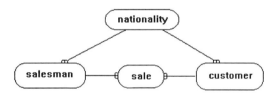

Since salesmen and customers may well be of differing nationalities, the nationality table will need to be brought into the joined set twice through the use of *aliases,* as shown overleaf. This action would break the *looped* nature of the joined set illustrated above, with which SQL cannot cope.

Another important use of aliases is described on page 15.

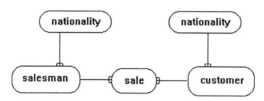

2.5 Views

Earlier in this chapter it was stated that the results of any piece of SQL are a subset of the rows and columns of the source table, or a set of joined tables. Indeed, the results could be stored in a new table and that table subsequently used as just another source table. Alternatively, the SQL can be stored away for reuse as a database *view*. The SQL can be reinvoked at any time and used in conjunction with any other piece of SQL by treating the view as if it were a table and adding it to the *select* statement list.

Although views are seen and handled just as if they were tables, they should never be mistaken for actual tables. The SQL which lies behind a view will be re-executed every time a query is executed that includes the view in its SQL. Because views are created for the very reason that their SQL is likely to be frequently reused, the amount of processing likely to be triggered by their underlying SQL should never be substantial. If it were (i.e. if the SQL behind a view is likely to take many minutes or even hours to execute), consideration ought to be given to the use of tables rather than views. Although such tables are usually referred to as *temporary* tables, they ought strictly to be called *derived* tables, since their contents are derived from data already existing in the database. Such tables would normally be populated on a regular basis and via overnight batch processes.

The classic use of derived tables is the creation of *aggregate* (or *statistical)* tables in which detailed data is summarized down into tables of fewer records and fewer attributes. Aggregate tables are the stuff of *data warehouses* and will be discussed further in Chapter 3. Note that if the aggregate table and the table (detailed) whose data was used to build it are both included in the same database, they can be joined as parent and child, respectively, with the aggregate table (parent) possibly sharing some of the child table's reference/parent tables.

2.6 Cartesian Products

SQL interpreters will not complain if two tables are referred to in the *from* clause of a piece of SQL without any associated matching criteria being present in the *where* clause. On the contrary, every row in one table will be matched against every row in the other, resulting in what is referred to as a *Cartesian product.* For example, if there were 1000 rows in one table and 500 in the other, the result would be 500,000 rows of output (assuming the absence of any record selection criteria).

Rather less obvious is the case of a parent table having two or more child tables, as illustrated on the right. Were these three tables to be joined in a single piece of SQL, with the two parent-child relationships included as matching criteria in the *where* clause, a *part*-Cartesian product would ensue between the *post offices* and *hotels* tables. Although the matching of the two child tables would be constrained by town (i.e. no hotel from, say, 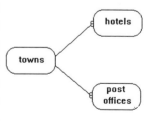 Leeds would be attempted to be matched against a post office from, say, Manchester), every post office in any given town would be matched against every hotel in the same town.

The situation would be worsened if the post offices or hotels were themselves parents of further tables. The truth is that wherever there are two or more childless tables in any given set of tables, the tables in that set would not be able to be *freely* joined in any *single* piece of SQL. Expressed the other way around, as long as there is only a single childless table in a given set of related tables, any number of tables in the set (including *all* of them) can be safely joined in any single piece of SQL.

CHAPTER 3

Data Modeling for Business Objects

$\mathbf{A}$n example of the *single childless table* structure described on the previous page is shown below and is more commonly referred to as a *star* or *snowflake* structure of which the childless table is the main focus or *master* table. To the Business Objects product, snowflake structures are crucial and referred to as *contexts*.

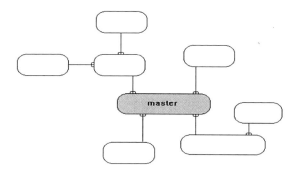

3.1 Contexts

Such structures are *safe* ones in that part-Cartesian products are avoided. Moreover, the group function dangers discussed in Section 2.3 (page 7) are also avoided so long as sum(), avg() and count() group function values are selected from the master table only.

In snowflake structures, all the non-master tables can be seen as the master table's *reference* or *look-up* tables. A given database structure can be segmented into several snowflake structures and each will have a master table. Some non-master tables will often be shared by the master tables of other snowflake structures.

An example is illustrated below where three (of several) snowflake structures, or contexts, have been identified within a source data model.

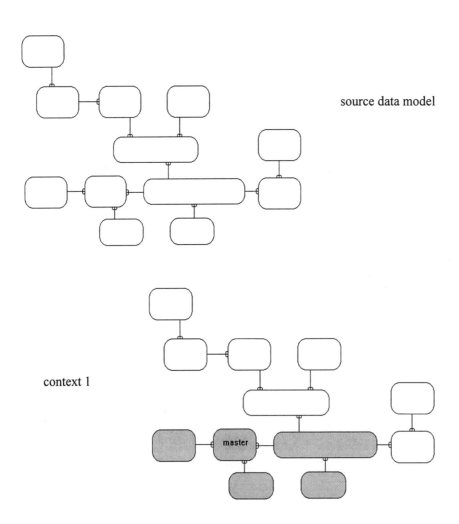

source data model

context 1

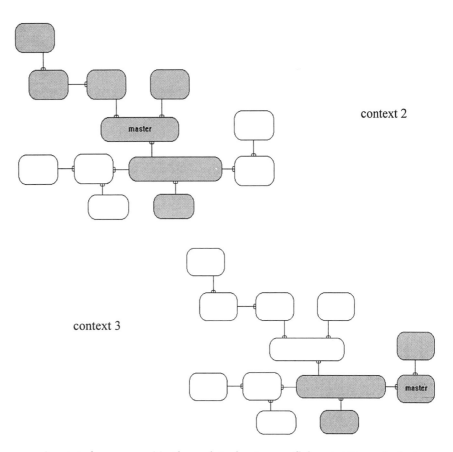

context 2

context 3

As stated on page 11, the point about snowflake structures is that any combination of their tables (including all of them) can be safely included in any *single piece* of SQL without the results showing any Cartesian behavior. Remember that the SQL interpreter will neither know nor care about the existence of part-Cartesian joins between the tables presented to it and will go ahead and produce a resulting set of rows and columns. Only if end users spot unusually large or small aggregate values in the results (or two or more descriptive items which although unrelated appear next to one another in the same result line) will suspicions be roused.

Note that a given table can only appear in one context as a master table. Note also that a table appearing as a master table must be differentiated from the same table where it appears in other contexts as a non master table. This is achieved by creating aliases on the table; one for the master and another for all its other, non master, manifestations (different non master manifestations of the same table do not need to be differentiated). Group functions are referenced to the master alias and non group functions (keys) with the non master alias. This will avert the group function dangers described on page 7.

3.2 Merging results

Although results from different contexts will need to be derived by separate pieces of SQL, Chapter 4 will explain how the Business Objects product (version 4) is able to automatically (and transparently to end users) process separate individual pieces of SQL in parallel, merging the results afterward into a single results set. Merging will be carried out upon common keys. For example, all three of the contexts illustrated earlier share the two tables shaded below.

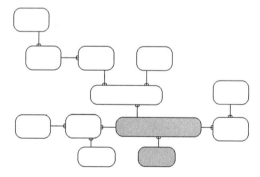

Results from each of the three contexts may well contain keys from one of these two tables and if they do, the result sets can be merged on those keys. An example is shown overleaf where two result sets, derived from different contexts, have been combined to form a third set.

TOWN	NO OF HOTELS	AREA (sq m)
Leeds	122	3.8
Manchester	186	5.1

TOWN	NO OF HOTELS	POPULATION
Leeds	122	854332
Bradford	93	453223

Merging the above would produce the following:

TOWN	NO OF HOTELS	AREA (sq m)	POPULATION
Leeds	122	3.8	854332
Manchester	186	5.1	
Bradford	93		453223

Note how unknown results are left blank (nulled) rather than given zero values (i.e. for group function values appearing in one table but not the other).

Note that when using version 3 of the Business Objects product, any merging of results from different contexts would have to be done manually and outside the realm of Business Objects tools. Version 3 end users will be warned whenever they attempt to incorporate tables from different contexts in the same SQL query. Version 4, however, will allow data items to be selected freely from different contexts for the same query. Business Objects will automatically run two or more separate SQL processes, transparently to users, and merge the results afterward.

Note that version 3 users who need to combine results from different queries can achieve it to some degree through the use of database *views* (see page 9). For example, the towns and post offices tables in the data model shown overleaf will clearly belong to one segment and the towns and hotels tables to another. The post offices table could effectively be brought into the towns-hotels segment by creating a view of it, keyed on town. The view can replace the table and since the view will have a *one-to-one* relationship with the towns table, it can safely become part of the towns-hotels segment.

The disadvantage of the view approach is that details are lost from the post offices table. Note, however, that the Oracle *decode* function can be used to salvage some of that detail. For example, if one of the attributes of the post offices table is service level ((F)ull, (M)edium or (N)one), the following statements will keep tabs on service levels by splitting total sales between them:

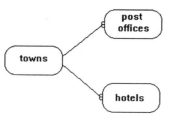

```
sum(decode(s_level,'F',sales,0),
sum(decode(s_level,'M',sales,0),
sum(decode(s_level,'N',sales,0)
```

Business end users will receive their Business Objects results in tabular form as rows and columns. Columns can be either non-numeric or numeric, and the former will usually be kept together and placed to the left of the latter. Non-numeric columns could be further sub divided into *keys* and *detail* columns. Keys could be identified by applying the rule that "any column which has substantially fewer distinct (unique) values than the total number of records in the results set can be regarded as keys".

An example of a *detail* column would be a surname of which there would almost be as many distinct values as there are rows.

Bear in mind, however, that *value* columns can be converted into keys by being arranged into *value ranges*. Age, for example, could be grouped into four or five age ranges and these treated as keys.

3.3 Hierarchies

The order in which keys are arranged, left to right, will usually (but not always) be regarded by end users as an indication of their hierarchical relationships. In other words, a given key will be a *parent* of the key to its right and a *child* to a key to its left. These hierarchical relationships are fundamental to the way in which end users will be able to analyze, and format into reports and charts, their results. For example, the way in which simple summary reports are sorted and break-totalled is hierarchically based.

In creating the end-user interfaces (Universes), Business Objects designers will often need to build into those interfaces an indication of hierarchical key relationships for the benefit of end users (please refer to Section 4.2).

From a relational data modeling point of view, an obvious hierarchy is one between parent and child tables. For example, in the joined pair of tables shown right, hotels can clearly be regarded as children (or subordinates) of towns.

However, hierarchical key relationships can also be found within a single table. For example, consider a classification code in the towns table which might have three possible (or *distinct*) values: (M)etropolitan area, (B)orough and (V)illage. This code can clearly be regarded as a parent of town.

Some keys will inevitably not be necessarily hierarchically related. In other words, they can be freely interchanged as parent and child. For example, *county* can be parent or child of the classification code (M, B or V) mentioned above. Another example is shown right comprising three joined tables. Town code and hotel group code are hierarchically interchangeable as parent and child. In these hierarchically ambiguous circumstances, the

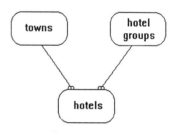

interface designer can indicate alternative hierarchical structures. Alternatively, interchangeable hierarchical structures are ideal for representation by matrix (or *crosstab*, in Business Objects terms), as illustrated overleaf.

	Holiday Inns	Hiltons
Leeds	122	35
Manchester	186	212
Bradford	93	80

There are many candidates for hierarchies in the snowflake structure shown below. Here are just some of them:

a,c,d   b,c,d   a,e   e,a   n,m,a   e,a,d

And here are some possible matrix arrangements:

a by b   c,d by n   a,e by g,h

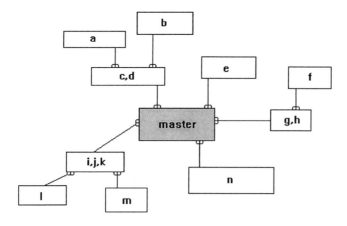

The most common use of hierarchies is in the production of *break reports*, such as, for example, one involving keys b, c and d (see previous page) and group functions sum(x) and avg(y), where x and y are *value* columns of the master table.

When using the Business Objects *Drill Down* tool (described in Section 6.2), end users will make particular use of hierarchies.

3.4 Aggregating

In the process of creating a query, business end users will decide what hierarchical structure they want and this will be reflected in the left-to-right arrangement of the non-numeric (*key*) attributes which appear in the tabular results of the query.

In many cases the results tables brought back from a query into the PC will be precisely what the user wanted and no further manipulation will be necessary. After all, when creating a query, users are allowed to select which attributes are to appear, their left-to-right arrangement, the record selection criteria and sorting instructions.

On the other hand, there a variety of ways in which results tables can be manipulated within the PC. These fall into four categories:

Slicing and Dicing
Drill-Down
Charting
Data Mining

Slicing and Dicing

Whatever the arrangement of the rows and columns of a given results table brought back by a query to the server database, that arrangement can be changed once the data arrives in the PC. And this can be done very rapidly since all the data is within the PC's memory.

i.e.   Columns can be switched around or removed altogether.
        Rows can be removed by applying further selection criteria.
        Rows can be resorted.
        Columns can be arranged into a matrix (crosstab).
        Breaks can be applied and break-totals created.

Drill-Down

For large volumes of data, fully detailed reports can be cumbersome to read on screen and to print out. A better solution is to present the results aggregated to the highest hierarchical key level but to be able to *break out selected* lines of results into the next hierarchical detail level and continue to *drill down* to further levels. Users can therefore *localize* the amount of detail to those records they wish to investigate further. For example, the initial results set (returned from the query) might show annual sales figures for a list of hotels. For hotels with unusually poor sales figures, further details (say, monthly figures) can be obtained. Similarly, for months with particularly poor figures, further details (say departmental breakdown) can be obtained.

Charts

Tables can be converted into a variety of pictorial charts (histograms, pie charts etc.) in two or three dimensions.

Data Mining

Data mining is the process of applying a variety of record selection criteria to a data set and searching amongst the resulting data sub-sets for ones with significant characteristics. In business terms, the aim is to identify patterns and trends, or derive target groupings for marketing purposes.

CHAPTER 4

The Business Objects Designer Module

Chapters 2 and 3 provide overviews on the subject of data modeling. The concepts expressed in those chapters need to be understood before attempting to use the Business Objects *Designer* tool, which is described here. The tool enables the IT professional to render relational database structures more meaningful to business end users. As well as converting table attributes into meaningful words or phrases, the whole concept of tables and their relationships are hidden from end users altogether and replaced by tabular views - the rows and columns with which users, especially spreadsheet users, are more familiar. The results of the Business Objects Designer's work will be a user *interface* - a "business view" of the database.

The user interface (which is described from the end user's point of view in Chapter 5) describes the database in terms of *universes, classes* and *objects. Objects* are individual data items which are grouped into *classes* for convenience. Classes are grouped into *universes*. Objects are of three types: *measure* objects (the numerical results of group functions such as sum() and count()), *dimension* objects (essentially the *keys* on which measure objects are aggregated) and *detail* objects which are subordinates of *dimension* objects and usually descriptive in nature.

Users will be able to create SQL queries without needing to know anything about SQL, or even to being aware that SQL is employed at all. Universes can be viewed by users as rows and columns and the results of queries as subsets of them. The universe's rows are reduced by the query's *where clause* and the columns by the query's *select clause*. Both where and select clauses are specified by end users in terms of the universe's *objects*.

To run *queries*, users will:

- Select the objects they wish to appear as result columns, arranged left to right.

- Declare any record selection criteria, by selecting *condition* objects.

- Declare ordering criteria, also by selecting objects and specifying whether ordering is to be ascending or descending.

Chapter 3 introduced the *Business Objects data model* which is essentially a modified version of the relational database model. Specifically, the database model is subdivided into *contexts,* with *aliases* and *shortcut joins* possibly being included in the process.

The Business Objects Designer tool provides what is essentially a GUI-based *intelligent drawing board* through which the Business Objects data model is drawn up and thereby declared to the Designer module. Once the Business Objects data model has been established, the *objects* by which the model will be viewed by end users can be created.

This chapter is thus divided into two sections:

4.1 Creating Business Objects Data Models

4.2 Creating Objects

4.1 Creating Business Objects Data Models

The *Designer* tool is a GUI-based PC software product, linked to the server database via SQL calls. Before anything can be achieved, a *Universe* must be opened or created. Each universe will have one Business Objects data model and a set of objects associated with it, the latter grouped into classes. Each universe must be associated with a particular server database. The *Designer* tool makes calls to the server database's *meta* data in order to pick up database table structures and offer them as pick-lists to make it easier for Designers to build Business Objects data models and construct objects.

The main *Designer* tool screen is shown below.

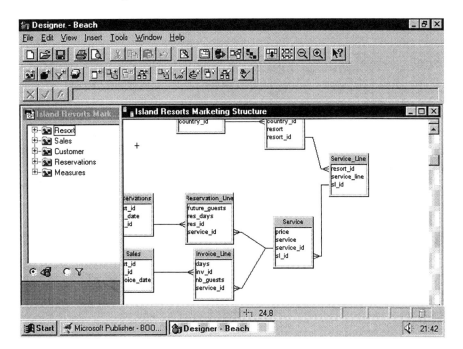

The screen consists of a variety of tool buttons at the top and a window below. In the window are two panes. On the right is the *drawing board* on which the data model (or *structure* in Business Objects terms) will appear as it is built up. As objects are created they will appear in the pane on the left.

The data model is built up in the following stages:

> Selecting tables
> Joining tables
> Indicating cardinalities
> Creating aliases
> Subdividing into contexts

4.1.1 Creating Tables

Tables are created by double-clicking the mouse button on any part of the drawing board or, alternatively, using the *tables* button shown on the right. The result will be the opening up of a window listing all the database tables. Double-clicking upon a table in the window will cause the table to appear on the drawing board where it can be resized and moved around.

Double-clicking on a table in the drawing board will cause its attributes to be temporarily hidden and the table size reduced to show the table name only. Double-clicking again will cause only those attributes involved with joins to other tables to be displayed. Double-clicking again will return to the original display in which all the table's attributes are shown.

Although the Business Objects Designer tool normally accesses table structures from the server database, it is also able to select data if necessary. This can occasionally help the designer to get a picture of the data he or she is dealing with. The data content of any table in the drawing board can be pulled across from the server database and viewed by clicking on a table to highlight it and selecting the *Table Values* option of the *View* menu option. The values will appear in a horizontally and vertically scrollable spreadsheet-like window.

These data windows can be opened up for several tables at the same time. Repeating rows in a window can be eliminated by ticking the window's *Distinct Values* box in its lower left corner.

Values for just one column of a table can be viewed by moving the mouse pointer over the column of interest in a table on the drawing board (where the pointer will change to a hand symbol), pressing the right mouse button and selecting the *View Column Values* option from the pop-up menu. The column's values will appear in a single column data window, which will also contain a *Distinct Values* tick-box for removing repeating values.

An alternative to looking at data values is to obtain row count and this is achieved in two ways. The first is to select the *Options* option of the *Tools* menu option and tick the *Show Row Count* box in the *Graphics* section, shown below.

This will cause row counts to be permanently displayed on the drawing board for every table in the data model.

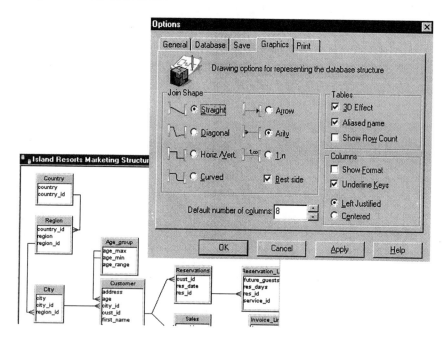

The second method is to select the *Number of Rows in Table* option of the *View* menu option, which opens up the following window:

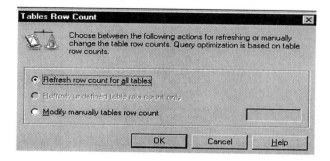

4.1.2 Joining Tables

Having placed a number of tables on the drawing board, the next stage is to join them together. Although it is recommended that this be done on a manual basis, it *is* possible to get the Designer tool to do it by activating the *Detect Joins* button (shown right). Without accessing a CASE database, however, all the joins wizard can do is look for similar column names between tables and presume them to be primary and foreign keys.

The idea (or *strategy*) of searching for identical column names, as employed by the joins wizard, is one of three *default strategies* available to the Designer tool for joining tables. These strategies can be viewed via the strategy tool button and strategy tab, shown below.

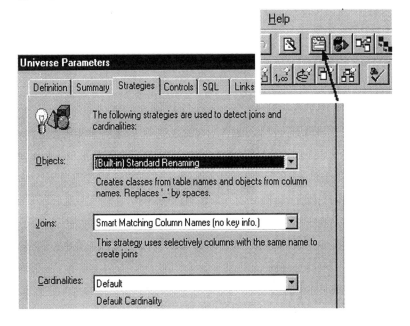

As stated earlier, it is suggested that joins be applied manually and this is achieved by positioning the mouse pointer over one of the attributes of a table in the drawing board, holding down the left mouse button and moving the mouse pointer across to an attribute of another table. On releasing the mouse button, the two tables will be joined by the attributes indicated.

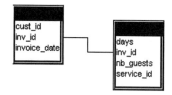

The join will be displayed graphically in the drawing board window, as shown above, and the corresponding piece of SQL (the *matching* or *join* criteria destined for incorporation into the SQL created, transparently, by end users in the building of their queries) can be seen by opening up the *list* frame via the *List Mode* option of the View pop-up menu, as shown left. The frame also shows tables and contexts (these will be discussed later on).

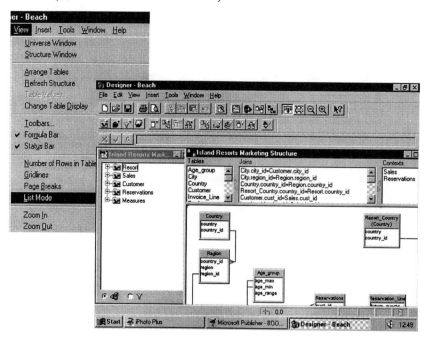

Outer joins can be specified by opening up the joins window (shown below) by double-clicking on any part of a join line in the drawing board.

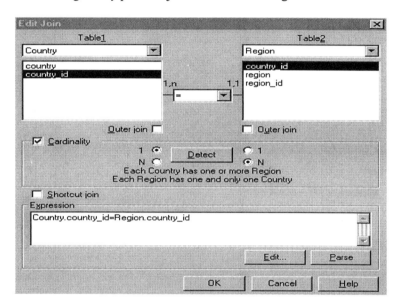

An outer join is specified by ticking the *outer join* box on the appropriate side of the join (i.e. the side indicated by the + sign on page 7). The SQL expression associated with the join is shown in the bottom of the window.

A *shortcut join* can be specified. The advantages of shortcut joins can be explained by considering the three joined tables below. Sometimes it is useful to carry a primary key not only into a child table (as foreign key), but through to the grand child table as well.

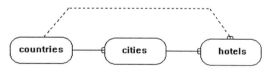

This act of denormalization is a pragmatic way of improving performance when attribute values from an intervening table (*cities*) are not required in a query. Shortcut joins are indicated in the data model by ticking the *Shortcut join* box in the join window.

4.1.3 Indicating Cardinalities

Table joins will usually be parent-child (one-to-many) relationships and it is important to identify which is the parent and which the child table in the join (i.e the *cardinality* of the join). Like joins, it is recommended that cardinalities be declared manually, even though the *Detect Cardinalities* tool button can be used 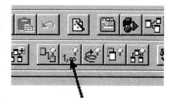 instead. Cardinalities are shown in the drawing board according to the graphics option in place at the time. The graphics options are shown on page 28. The default style is shown left.

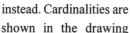

Cardinalities are established manually by double-clicking on a join within the drawing board. This will open up the join window, shown on the previous page. The cardinality is indicated by ticking the 1 and N buttons in the center of the window (1 indicating the *one* and N the *many* of a one-to-many relationship). A narrative will appear at the bottom of the window, describing in words the nature of the relationship.

Note incidentally that the drawing board window can be enlarged and reduced in scale, using the *Zoom* buttons (shown right). The drawing board can also be split, using the *Split* option of the *Windows* menu option, into two sections that can be scaled independently.

4.1.4 Creating Aliases

The use of aliases is described on pages 8 and 15. Aliases are created in the Designer tool by positioning the mouse pointer on a table for which an alias is required to be created and pressing the right mouse button. A menu panel (shown right) will appear from which the *Insert Alias* option is selected. The important thing to be aware of is that whenever an alias is required for a table, the table itself must be removed from the data model but not from the drawing board. This means that *two* aliases will generally need to be created. While the aliases need to be joined to their respective tables, the aliased table will need to be disconnected from all other tables and, for tidiness and clarity, moved away from the model into a corner of the drawing board.

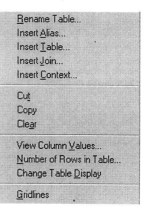

The *Detect Aliases* button can be used to get the Business Objects Designer tool to identify aliases.

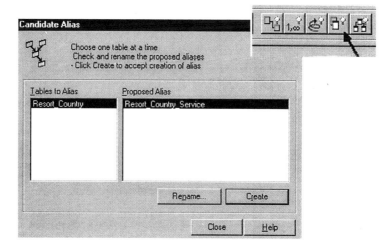

Bear in mind that the need for aliases is to eliminate loops in the data model. The *Detect Loops* button (shown right) can be used to get the designer tool to search for them.

4.1.5 Indicating Contexts

Chapter 3 describes the need to subdivide the database into safe segments or *snowflake structures*. These are referred to in the Designer tool as *contexts*. A context is a subset of the overall data model from which any number of tables (including all of them) can be safely incorporated into a query without any part-Cartesian products ensuing. An example is shown below.

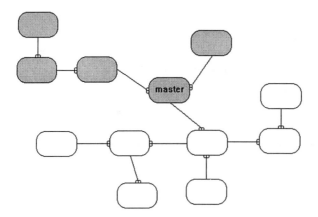

A context will contain only one childless table and this can be referred to as the *master* table with all the other tables being its reference or parent tables. All group-function values should be based on the master table, with the following exceptions:

```
count(distinct ..)
max()
min()
sum(master table attribute/reference table attribute)
sum(master table attribute * reference table attribute)
```

The Designer tool has a *Detect Contexts* button (shown right), although its findings may need to be modified.

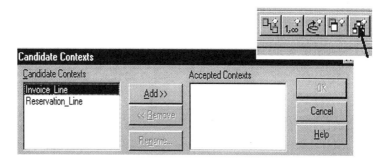

To recap on Section 4.1: a relational data model is made known to the Business Objects Designer tool by creating a pictorial representation of it on screen, selecting tables from pick-lists derived from the database's meta data, pulled across from the remote server. By selecting a table, it will appear in the window of the designer tool together with a list of its attributes. Relationships between tables, and their cardinalities, are declared by the user through simple point-and-click actions using the mouse. Users are able to cater for SQL alias constructs by creating alias tables in the pictorial data model. Users are also able to subdivide a pictorial data model into separate snowflake structures, taking advantage of the fact that the Designer tool will never attempt to include tables from different snowflake structures in the same piece of generated SQL; and thus avoiding the risk of Cartesian products.

4.2 Creating Objects (the end-user Interface)

Once the Business Objects data model has been established and made known to the Designer tool, objects can be created around it. These objects will be the business end users' only view of the data model, and hence their view of the server database that lies behind it.

Objects are essentially pieces of SQL; the building blocks with which the SQL behind end user's queries will be built. An object will usually correspond to one of the items in the *select* clause of a piece of SQL, and thus an attribute of a database table. On the other hand, an object might be a concatenation of two or more attributes or the results of group functions. If end users select objects based on the attributes of different tables, the Business Objects software will automatically (and transparently to users) add the table-join SQL into the query.

Objects are grouped into *classes* for convenience and classes can themselves be grouped as sub classes of other classes - all for no reason other than convenience and clarity. In general, a class will correspond to a database table and its objects to the table's attributes.

There are three types of object:

measure	The numerical results of group functions (sums, averages, counts, etc)
dimension	The *keys* on which *measure* objects are based
detail	Objects subordinate to *dimension* objects which will not be used as *measure* object keys

Measure and *dimension* objects should not be mixed together within classes.
Detail objects would not be selected along with measure
objects for the same query. In the Objects window,
shown right, object type is indicated by icon shape.

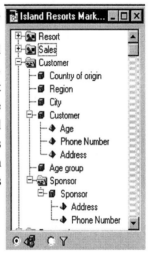

The objects are arranged in the classic hierarchical
manner seen in many of today's software products.
Clicking on the plus box will reveal the members of that
branch of the hierarchical tree, clicking again on the
minus box (which has now replaced the plus box) will
stop the branch members being displayed, the minus
sign reverting to a plus. Double-clicking on any item
will enable its details to be viewed and edited, as
described below.

4.2.1 Classes

Before an object can be created, the class into which it is to be placed must
already exist. New classes are created via the *Insert Class* button, shown below.

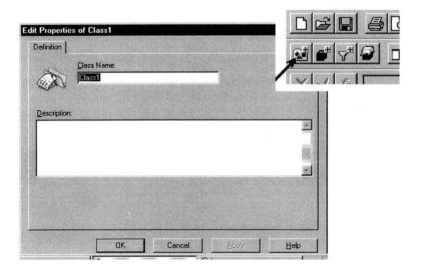

If the class is to be positioned after an existing class, the latter is clicked in the objects and classes window. A class name and description are entered into the classes window.

4.2.2 Objects

To create objects, the *Insert Object* button is used to open up the object editor window shown below. The same window can be obtained by double-clicking one of the existing objects in the classes and objects window.

The name and type of the object is entered together with a full description which will be displayed to end users.

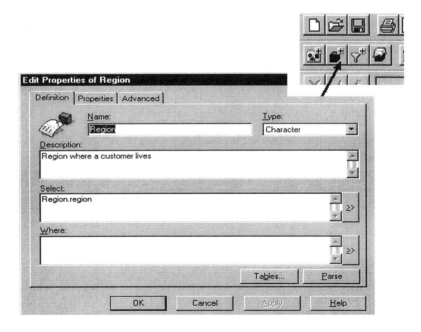

The *select* box is where the SQL associated with the object is declared. Although this can be keyed in manually, it is better to get the Designer tool to help by clicking on the edit button (shown right). This will open up the SQL editor window, also shown below.

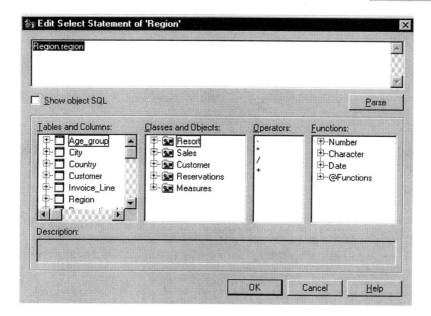

A column of a table (of the data model) can be selected from the window pane on the left by double-clicking it. Operators and functions can be selected from the two righthand window panes (classes and objects being second from left) together with the *Show object SQL* tick-box.

Typical *Select* statements are:

```
country.name
city.population
sum(city.population)
employee.initial||' '||employee.surname
employee.salary + employee.expenses
sum(employee.others * employee.rate)
count(distinct ucase(employee.surname))
```

and each will be given object names meaningful to the business end user, for example (respectively):

```
country name
city's population
Total population of cities
employee's name
employee's costs
employees' overtime costs
number of employees
```

Note that an alternative to keying SQL into the *select* window is to copy the *select* SQL of another existing object. This is achieved with the use of the **@select** function whose parameter is the name of the object (including its class name) whose SQL is being copied:

```
@select(classname\objectname)
```

The **@select** function is picked from the right most window pane and its parameter from the *Classes and Objects* pane (second from left).

This copying of existing SQL could be regarded as an *object-oriented* approach in that code is being reused.

4.2.3 Condition objects

Returning to the object *Edit Properties* window on page 39, note that there is an opportunity to apply a *where clause* statement. It is recommended that this be used rarely, not least for the reason that record selection criteria ought to be the concern of end users when creating queries. The main reason, however, can be seen when considering what happens when an end user selects several objects for a query, each of which includes a where clause. Such multiple where clauses can be mutually destructive, bearing in mind that the selection criterion of each object will be ANDed together in the resulting query's SQL. For example, if an object whose where clause includes `status_code = 'A'` is combined with another whose where clause includes `status_code = 'B'`, the resulting where clause will be `status_code = 'A' and status_code = 'B'` which will plainly result in a fruitless search. Identical where clauses can of course be combined safely. The resulting SQL will be visually unpleasing but no less efficient, and in any case is transparent to users.

It must be reiterated that hard-coded conditions should be avoided where possible and conditioning left to end users who are able to apply conditions in two ways. The simplest way is by the application of *simple conditions* and these are described in Section 4.2.5 and on page 62. The second way is by providing them with *condition* objects which they can freely select for their queries. For example, a condition object named "*new recruits*" might have the following SQL associated with it:

```
employee.type = 'N'
```

Condition objects (as opposed to the *select* objects described thus far) are created by clicking on the class under which the object is to be assigned and activating the *insert condition* button. This will open up the *edit condition properties* window shown overleaf.

The window is similar to the *Edit Properties* window shown on page 39 except that the *select* box is missing.

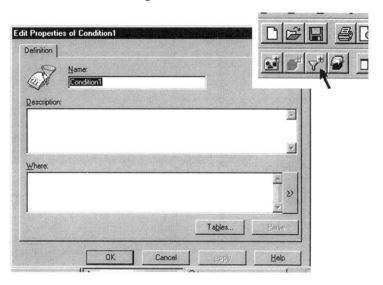

An alternative to actually keying in a piece of SQL into the where clause window is to copy the same where clause SQL as another existing object. This is achieved with the use of the @where function whose parameter (like that of the @select function described on page 41) is the name of the object (including its class name) whose SQL is being copied:

```
@where(classname\objectname)
```

Note, however, that, ironically, the object named as the parameter cannot be a condition object but must be a select object, of type *dimension*. Thus, if it is planned to adopt an object oriented approach in which a library of commonly used where clauses is set up, a class of *dimension* objects can be established, each having a where clause SQL but no *select* SQL. To stop users selecting these as select objects, the class can be hidden

from end users using the *show/hide item* button (shown right). The select objects will now need to be presented as condition objects and this is achieved by creating a corresponding set of condition objects, each of whose select definition will be a `@select` function whose parameter is one of the hidden objects.

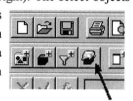

4.2.4 Interactive queries

An alternative to end users having to add, remove or change a query's conditions between reruns of the query is to be able to keep the same basic condition in place but make it possible for users to vary its parameters *interactively*, in other words, replacing the hard-coded conditional value, or values, with variable ones that will be prompted for by the query when run. These prompted values are equivalent to the run parameters supplied to report programs and are particularly useful when *ready written* queries are built by the Designer and supplied to end users. Such queries will (or should) be supplied with *user guides* in which any required parameters will be specified (supplying ready-made queries is a good way to help end users come to grips with the art of query building since they will be free to copy and change the queries supplied to them, and thus learn by example).

Variable conditions are made possible with the use of the special Business Objects function **@prompt**, which takes the following five parameters, only the first being mandatory:

1   The prompt message, in single quotes.

2   The variable's type, also in quotes:

          either of: A (character)
                         N (numeric)
                         D (date)

3   Either:

A bracketed list of values, each in single quotes and separated by commas. These will be presented to the end user as a *pick-list*.

or

The name of an existing object in the format shown below. The result will also be a list of values, resulting from the execution of the SQL behind the object. See Section 4.2.5 page 47 on the subject of *lists of values* (pick lists) associated with objects.

```
`classname\objectname`
```

4   Either `mono` or `multi`, indicating that the prompt will accept a single value only or several values.

5   Either `free` or `constrained`, the latter indicating that the end user *must* select from the list of values presented, as opposed to the former which indicates that users are free to enter any values they choose, irrespective of whether pick-lists are presented or not.

Note that once a `@prompt` function has been written into an object's definition, it needn't be repeated in any other's. This is achieved through the use of the Business Objects' `@variable` function whose parameter is the message text (the first parameter) of the `@prompt` function being borrowed. Like Business Objects **@select** and **@where** functions, this follows the principles of the object oriented approach where code is reused.

There are two special Business Objects variables whose values are constant and assigned automatically. These are BOUSER (the username associated with the current session) and BOPASS (the user's password).

The *Tables* button of the *edit object Properties* window, shown on page 39, is used to *force* a table to be included in a query's SQL, despite the fact that none of the objects selected for the query make reference to the table in their SQL. One reason for doing this might be to apply a *pseudo condition* to the query by bringing into the query's joined tables another table with the effect that only those records with matching records in the added table (perhaps a list of authorized people) will survive the join. The *Tables* button will open up a window of all available database tables. Those already referred to in the SQL will be highlighted. To bring other tables into the SQL, the control key is depressed while they are highlighted.

The *Parse* button is used to get the Designer tool to check the validity of the SQL behind the object. It will achieve this by accessing the server database.

Note that the objects window (shown on page 39) has three aspects to it, indicated by the tabs at the top of the window. So far the *Definition* aspect has been described. Clicking on the *Properties* tab reveals the window shown below. In the upper part of the window the object type can be declared (or *qualification* in Business Objects terms).

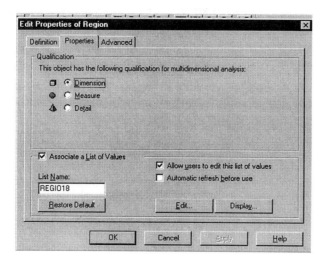

In the illustration, the *Dimension* type has been selected. Were the *Measure* type ticked, an additional data-entry box will appear, as shown below, into which the group function can be selected.

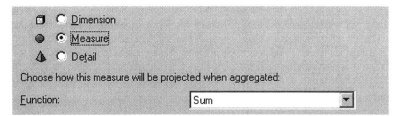

Were *Detail* selected, a different data-entry box would appear, as shown below, into which the dimension object with which this detail object is associated can be declared.

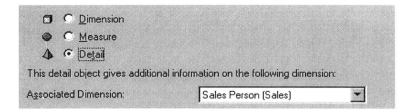

4.2.5 Lists of values

The lower part of the *Properties* tab of the Object window (see page 46) concerns *lists of values* (LOVs). These are the pick-lists which end users can use as an aid to data-entry when they apply *simple conditions* (see pages 42 and 62). Rather than manually keying object values when constructing conditions for their queries, end users can open up pick-lists and select values instead.

Every object is automatically given a *default* LOV, provided the *Associate a List of Values* box is ticked in the Properties window (*Condition* objects only). The default LOV is nothing more than the results of a query whose SQL consists solely of the object's own SQL. Just like those of queries, LOV results are preserved indefinitely on the user PC's disk and overwritten every time the LOV is *refreshed* (equivalent to the query being reexecuted).

The default query behind an object's default LOV can be changed. For example, conditions can be applied or additional *select* objects added. The procedure for changing the *query* behind a LOV is similar to that of an end user changing one of his or her own queries. On activating the *Edit* button in the LOV area of the Properties window (shown on page 46), the same query-building window used by end users will appear (see section 5.1).

The default queries behind LOVs are very simple, consisting of the object itself appearing in the select panel (and no conditions). A common enhancement of LOV queries is to add some meaningful text to the pick-list that appears to end users. For example, the default LOV of a *country code* object would present to the end-user no more than a list of country codes. It would be more useful to display actual country names alongside, or instead of, them

Note that it is often advantageous to include the `@prompt` function in the condition of the query behind a LOV. This would give end users the opportunity to modify the content of their pick-lists i.e. to reduce pick-list sizes by removing irrelevant members. In pressing the *Refresh* button in the pick-list window, end users will be prompted for a condition parameter.

The two remaining tick-boxes in the LOV panel of the object window are for:

- Allowing end users to alter the queries behind LOVs.
- Forcing the LOV's query to be reexecuted every time it is invoked by end users, thereby ensuring that the lists of values they see are always up to date.

The third tab (*Advanced*) of the object window is shown below. The top and bottom areas will be discussed in Chapter 9.

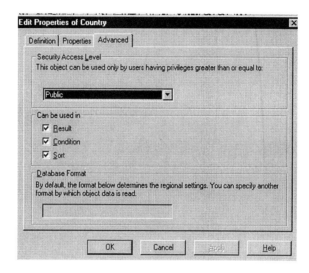

The middle area is where the usage of the object is declared. Ticking the *Result, Condition and Sort* boxes indicates how end users are allowed to make use of them when building queries.

4.2.6 Aggregate Awareness

It is clear that for large volumes of data, the results of group functions will necessarily involve much processing time, especially if several tables need to be joined together. In Chapter 2 it was suggested that processing times can be reduced by pre-aggregating the data and assembling it into *derived* tables. The results of sums, averages and counts could thus be selected straight out of such tables rather than have to be derived..

As an example, consider three joined tables of states, cities and streets. To derive the sum of the lengths of the streets of Ohio, or for each city of Ohio, would clearly involve a considerable amount of processing time. This could be reduced by creating a table of prederived sums of street lengths against city and state, and using the new table in place of the old *streets* table.

But what if end users want to keep the detailed streets table, with all its rich variety of attributes (street name, construction type, material type, etc). More to the point, what if end users sometimes want to derive sums of street lengths against a city or state, and at other times against, say, street construction type? The problem for the designer is that the *measure* object *sum of street lengths* cannot be based on both the old (detailed) streets table *and* the new (aggregate) streets table. Having two objects with almost similar names will confuse end users. For example, how will they know not to select an aggregate-based *measure* object together with a non-aggregate-based *dimension* object (say, construction type), and vice versa.

Business Objects comes to the rescue with its *aggregate awareness* facility. This provides the ability to:

(a)   Assign two or more alternative definitions of an object, and prioritize them. For example, the definition of the *sums of street lengths* object could be defined as:

first choice: sum(aggregate_table.slength)
second choice: sum(detail_table.slength)

(b)   Define, for each aggregate table, the objects allowed to be selected into the same query. For example, declare all the *dimension* objects of states and cities to be allowed to be used in association with the aggregate table.

End users will then be free to select the *sums of street lengths* object and leave Business Objects with the decision of which streets tables to use. Business Objects will look at the collection of objects selected for the query and decide whether they *all* fall within the allowable set for the aggregate streets table. If not, the software will use the second option of each of the *measure* objects. Note that any number of aggregate tables can be introduced into the database. Note also that more than one aggregate table can be associated with the same detailed table (in which case there will be more than two alternative definitions of associated *measure* objects).

(a) and (b) above are carried out as follows.

(a)   The prioritized list of alternative *measure* object definitions are entered into the *select* box of the object definition window as parameters of the special function **@aggregate_aware()**

(b)   The objects allowed (or rather *not* allowed) to be used in conjunction with a given aggregate table are declared in the window shown below, which is obtained via the *Aggregate Navigation* option of the Tools menu. Note that it is the incompatible objects that are ticked in the right hand window.

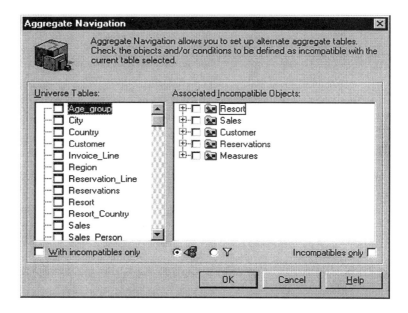

4.2.7 Hierarchies and Drill-down

On page 37 the three types (or *qualifications*) of object were described together with an explanation of how *dimension* objects are used in conjunction with *measure* objects. This is because the *dimension* objects are effectively the *keys* on which the measures are calculated, or *aggregated*. Thus, for example, if *dimension* objects *country of origin* and *city,* and *measure* object *population count* were selected, the result would be a population count for each distinct combination of country of origin and city.

Note that the two dimension objects in the example above happen to be hierarchically related to one another in that a country will have several cities associated with it. Hierarchically related objects are prime candidates for *master-detail* (or *break*) reporting.

On the other hand, two objects of, for example, nationality and age group (relating to employees) have a *many-to-many* relationship in that there are likely to be several nationalities of employee falling within a particular age group and, conversely, several age groups falling within a particular nationality. In other words, there are two alternative hierarchical structures involving age group and nationality, making these objects prime candidates for *crosstab* (or *matrix*) reporting and *master-detail* reporting alternatives.

In order to use the Business Objects end-user *Drill-Down tool* (described in Section 6.2) end users must be provided (by the designer) with indications of the hierarchical relationships between objects. This is achieved by clicking on the *Hierarchies* button and opening up the hierarchies editing window, shown overleaf.

The left side of the two window panes is the classes and objects window. Into the right most pane can be assembled hierarchical lists (or *hierarchies*). These will be displayed in much the same manner as the classes and objects, with folders representing hierarchies rather than classes and blue cubes representing its members (because they will all be *dimension* objects). And in the same way classes must be created before their objects, hierarchies must be created before theirs.

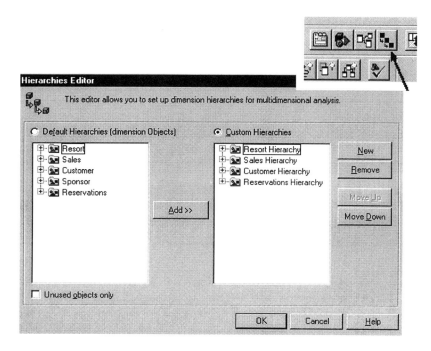

To move an object from the left pane into a hierarchy is just a matter of either dragging it across, or highlighting one or more objects and clicking on the *Add* button. Note that objects from different classes can be added to the same hierarchy. Note also that the same object can be added to several hierarchies. For example, two hierarchies might contain the same set of objects but arranged in different order. An object can be repositioned vertically by placing the mouse pointer on it and, while holding the left mouse button down, dragging the object over another object. The dragged object will reappear below the one over which it was moved.

The hierarchies established here by the designer will become available to end users who use the Drill-Down tool (described in Section 6.2).

Note that designers should always make the effort to create *Universe Guides* for use by end users in which Universes are described in detail and in business terms.

To recap on Section 4.2: business users can be presented with group function items referred to in Business Objects terms as *measure* objects; and non-group-function items referred to in Business Objects terms as *dimension* and *detail* objects. These can be arranged into groups referred to in Business Objects terms as *classes*. *Dimension* objects are the keys on which the aggregated data of group_funtions are based.

Source data models can be subdivided into what in Business Objects terms are referred to as *Universes* or *contexts*. The Universe approach is recommended for Business Objects version 3 users, who will be prevented from selecting objects from different Universes for the same query. Query results from different Universes will have to be merged manually, and outside the Business Objects product. Using *contexts*, version 3 users will receive error messages when they attempt to select objects from different contexts for the same query. These messages will be confusing for business end users and the context approach is not advised in version 3 .

Version 4 of the Business Objects product, however, is powerful and its users are able to freely select objects for the same SQL process, whatever context they belong to. Users will be able to run a single query (or what will appear to them as a single query) across two or more contexts and receive a single set of results. Version 4 in any case includes PC-based end-user tools enabling users to merge two or more result sets (i.e results from different SQL processes) after they have been produced.

CHAPTER 5

User Tools - Reporting

$\mathbf{E}$nd users are able to create and maintain database queries and store their results in their PCs. Queries can be re-run at any time, overwriting (or *refreshing*) any previously obtained results from the same query. Queries can be changed, or copied and changed, to produce new queries.

Although the results of a query can be viewed in a results window of the query building tool, they are best looked at in the form of *reports* in which the data is formatted into tables and charts along with accompanying titles and column headers. Such formatting can involve re-arranging columns, applying row deselection criteria, re-sorting rows, arranging into crosstabs (matrices) and producing graphical representations (or *charts*) such as pie charts and histograms. In other words, the trip from server database to PC is only the first leg of the journey from database to business end-user.

Reports are contained within *documents*, each document corresponding to a physical computer file. Several reports can be contained within the same document. A report can span across several pages of its document, although each individual report will start on a new page.

Note that PC end-users who have no access to any relational databases, whether remotely or locally based, can still make use of the Business Objects end-user tools described in chapters 5 through 8 by directing them towards any data files held in their PC. As long as the file's records are structured consistently as *rows and columns*, the Business Objects tools will simply regard them as if they were the results of database queries.

5.1 Database Queries

Business Objects end users will have been provided, by the *Designer*, with one or more *Universes*. Each Universe will comprise a number of *objects*, arranged into *classes* for convenience. Possibly unknown to the end user, each object is essentially a piece of SQL; a building block which can be combined with others to form a complete SQL statement or *query*. When the query is *run*, the SQL statement is sent across to the server database and executed there, bringing the results back to the PC as a set of rows and columns which are stored on the PC's disk. Whenever the query is rerun, the results in the PC are overwritten or *refreshed*. The rows and columns of query results can be viewed directly on screen or, preferably, copied into *reports* where they can be reformatted, filtered, sorted and arranged into a whole range of presentational formats.

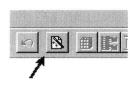

Before a query can be constructed, a report must be created to receive its results. This is achieved via the reports wizard, invoked by the tool button shown left. The reports wizard is described on page 76, and one of its screens prompts the user to open a *Universe* (shown below).

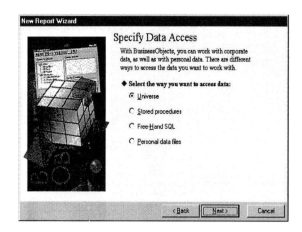

The screen presents a pick-list of available universes.

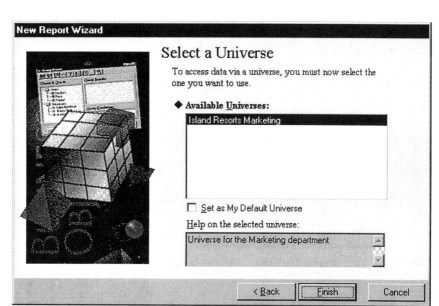

Selecting one and clicking the *Finish* button invokes the query builder screen, shown overleaf.

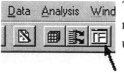 The query-building screen can alternatively be invoked, to modify existing queries (i.e. behind existing reports), using the *Data Provider* button shown left.

The query builder screen is divided into three windows. In the left window are the objects available in the Universe, arranged into classes. This window can be removed/reintroduced using button A shown right. The folders can be opened out to reveal their constituent objects. Full business descriptions of highlighted objects can be caused to appear at the bottom of the screen by using button B shown right.

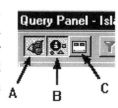

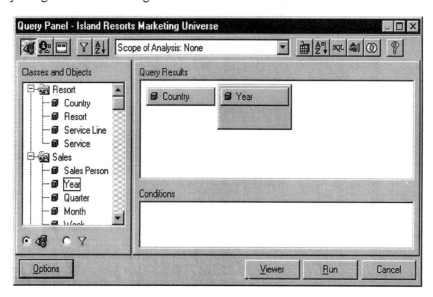

5.1.1 Result Objects

The top right window (the *Query Results* window) is where objects (*Select* objects) selected from the left window can be assembled and these will form the *columns* of the query results, appearing in the same left to right order in which they have been assembled. If there are too many objects to fit horizontally in the *Query results* window, button C (shown above right) can be used to cause them to "wrap" into two or more lines.

Note that the *Year* object icon in the Query results area has a "back panel", unlike the *Country* icon. This simply indicates that Year is the object currently highlighted (clicking on the *Country* object will transfer the back panel to it). Note

that one or more of the result objects in the Query results area can be declared as *sort keys* simply by highlighting the object and clicking on the *sort* button, shown left. Double-clicking the sort icon, which will have appeared in the object panel, will reverse it from ascending to descending.

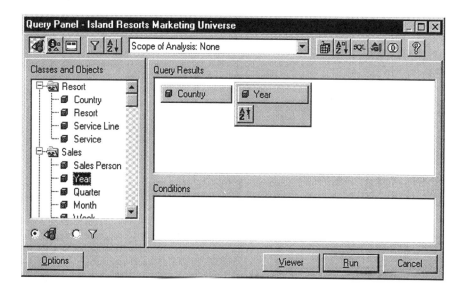

Note that if a sort is now applied to *County*, without removing the sort on *Year*, rows will be sorted in County within Year - in other words the sorting will be applied in the order in which the sorts were applied to the objects.

The order in which sorts are applied is not evident in the query builder screen but can be examined, and changed, through the use of the *Manage Sorts* button shown right. This will open up the sort manager panel below that.

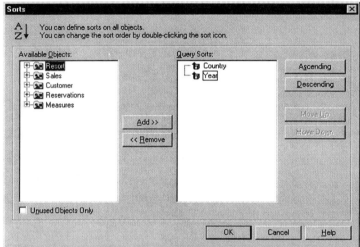

The sort objects are shown in the right window and are applied from top to bottom. This vertical ordering can be changed by clicking on a sort object in the right window and using the *Move Up* or *Move Down* buttons to the lower right of the panel. The sorts can be changed from ascending to descending and vice versa using the buttons on the right. Sort objects can be added and removed using the buttons in the center of the panel, available objects being presented in the left window.

5.1.2 Condition Objects

Moving on from *result* objects to *condition* objects, the right most of the two buttons in the lower left corner of the query builder screen (page 58) can be clicked to replace the *result* objects with *condition* objects in the left hand window of available objects.

In the screen shown below, the *Resort* and *Customer* class folders have been opened up and two objects moved into the *Conditions* window.

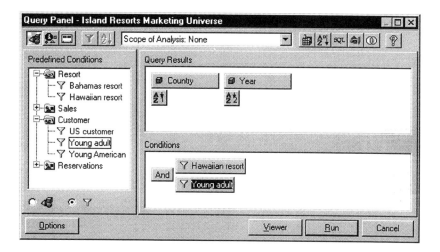

Note how an *and* or *or* has been automatically inserted between them. Double clicking on the *and* icon will change it to an *or,* and vice versa. Doing this when there are three or more condition objects will cause some of them to be indented. Examples are shown below.

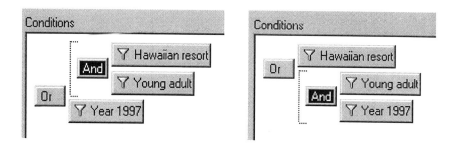

A desired conditional structure can be obtained by a combination of double-clicking *and*s into *or*s (and vice versa), cancelling indentation and switching the relative vertical positions of the condition objects. Indentations are cancelled by placing the mouse pointer on a condition object, holding down the left mouse button and sliding the object to the left (some *or*s will be changed to *and*s, or vice versa, in the process). The relative vertical positions of objects can be changed (as long as none are indented) by placing the mouse pointer on a condition object, holding down the left mouse button and sliding the object up or down over neighboring objects. *Condition* objects can be removed from the *Conditions* window altogether by highlighting and using the *Delete* keyboard key.

Note that some conditions will prompt end users for conditional values (see page 44) when queries are run. Note that all such prompts should be warned about in the *Universe User Guides* produced by Designers for end users in which all the objects (both *result* and *condition*) in all the Universes supplied to end users will be described.

Still on the subject of conditions, what in Business Objects terms are referred to as *simple conditions* can be applied to *result* objects through the use of pick-lists (or, in Business Objects terms *Lists of values* which are discussed on pages 43 and 47). This is achieved by highlighting a result object (in the Query results window) and clicking on the *Filter* button, shown right. This will invoke a pick-list of candidate values. Double-clicking as item will apply the value to the condition.

Although many end users will have no interest in the SQL which lies behind their queries (and may not even understand what SQL is), it can be revealed via the SQL button at the top of the screen. For the query shown in the panel below, the resulting SQL is shown in the panel below it, and continued overleaf.

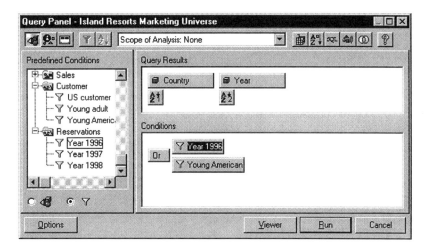

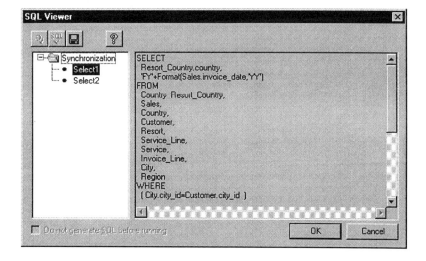

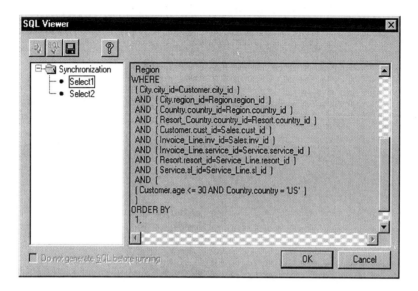

Note the construction of the result objects, the join conditions (applied automatically by Business Objects), the conditions specified in the query builder screen and the ordering.

5.1.3 Scope of Analysis (for Drill down)

The Business Objects *Drill-Down* tool is described in Section 6.2 and also mentioned in Chapter 4, page 52. The Drill-Down tool will not operate unless the query builder has prepared the way for it. Specifically, a query needs to be built which delivers "hidden keys", that is, one or more *result* objects which, despite not appearing in the Query results window at the top of the query-builder screen, are nonetheless delivered to the end users PC. Once they have arrived there, users will be able to reveal them using the Drill-Down tool.

The objects which *are* placed in the Query Results window and those which are not (but returned by the query nonetheless) must all be members of the same class or *hierarchy*. A *hierarchy* is simply a set of objects, much like a class but created by the Universe designer to indicate a sequence of objects which can be considered hierarchically related in the the order in which they appear in the hierarchical list. (page 66 describes how to find out which hierarchies are available in a Universe).

The *result* objects that are placed into the *Query Results* window must all be members of the same *hierarchy*, or class, must be contiguous members (i.e. no objects missing between the first and last) and arranged in the same order (left to right) as they appear (top to bottom) in the hierarchy or class list. The *result* objects which are to be "delivered under wraps" will be one or more of those which immediately follow (in the hierarchy or class) the last object placed into the Query Results window.

For example, suppose a hierarchy (or class) contains the following objects:

Year, Month, Country, State, City, Region, Store

and suppose the query-builder wishes to explicitly deliver objects *Country* and *State* and accompany them with hidden versions of objects *City* and *Region*. This is achieved by placing the *Country* and *State* objects into the Query results window, then highlighting the right most object (*State*) and clicking the button at the right side of the *Scope of Analysis* window right at the top of the query builder screen.

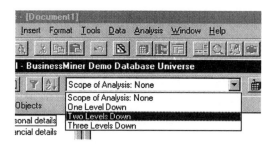

Selecting *Two Levels Down* will cause two further objects (i.e. *City* and *Region)* to be implicitly delivered to the end user.

An alternative way of achieving the same result, and also to see what *hierarchies* are available in the *Universe*, is to use the *Scope of Analysis* button, shown right. The resulting panel is shown overleaf.

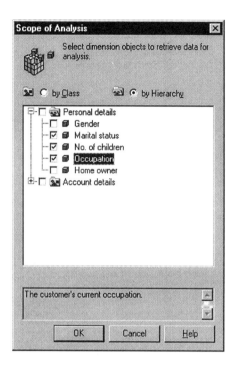

Note how either hierarchies or classes can be selected to be presented and how when a class or hierarchy is opened out (by clicking on the +), the objects selected (both explicit and hidden) are indicated.

5.1.4 Combining Queries

On page 15 it was stated that Business Objects version 4 enables end users to
run two or more separate queries and combine the
results into a single results set (or report). This is
achieved by clicking the button shown right to obtain
another query-builder panel. Separate queries will
appear as separate tabs along the bottom of the screen (see below). Result objects
from the first query (or the query in focus when the button was clicked) will appear
in the new query's *Query Results* window (although the *Conditions* window will be
emptied). This is because any two or more queries whose results are to be combined
must share at least one common key (*dimension* object) in order for them to be
combined. Thus, although some of the result dimension objects copied from the first
query can be removed from the new query (and new result and condition objects
added), at least one of the copied objects must remain.

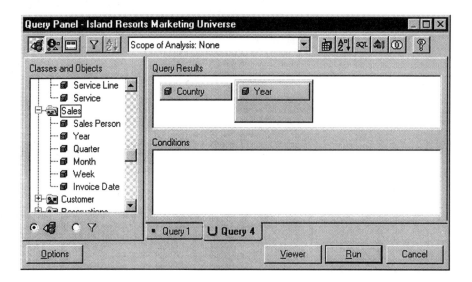

5.1.5 User Objects

End users can build their own "personal" (or *user*) objects out of the objects supplied to them in the Universe by using the *User Objects* button shown right. The panel shown below it will be invoked showing any user objects already created. Clicking on its *Add* button will invoke the panel shown below that.

As an example, an object for average sales revenue has been created, of type numeric and measure, and the *avg* function specified at the bottom of the panel.

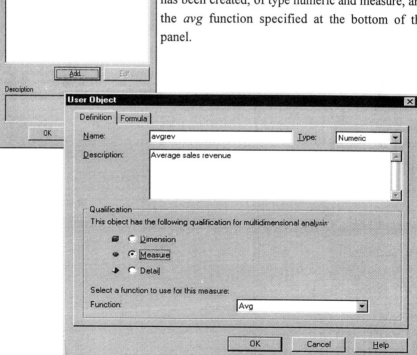

Were type *Detail* to have been selected (instead of *measure*), a prompter for
an associated *Dimension* object would be presented as shown below.

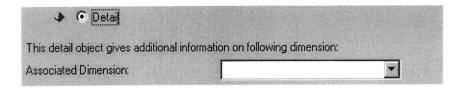

Clicking on the *Formula* tab at the top of the main panel will invoke the panel
shown below in which the new object can be constructed, taking an object from the
Classes and Objects window and a formula or operator from the other two
windows.

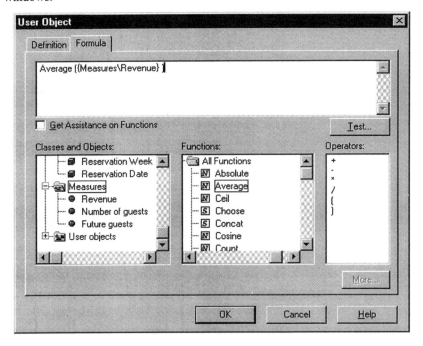

The *Test* button can be used to get Business Objects to check the
function for correctness.

Ticking the *Get Assistance on Functions* button will cause a whole range of assistance screens to appear, depending on the function selected.

5.1.6 General Query Options

Clicking on the *Options* button in the lower left corner of the Query Builder screen (shown on page 58) will invoke the panel below.

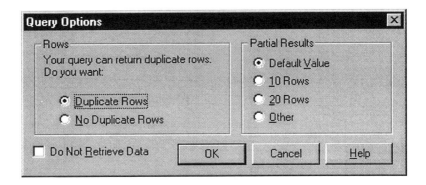

The *No Duplicate Rows* button on the left will remove all but one of every set of rows whose column values are all identical.

Ticking the *Do Not Retrieve Data* box will enable queries to be checked by Business Objects against the server database when run, but without retrieving any data.

The *Partial Results* area on the right enables Business Objects to stop query processing after a specified number of rows have been retrieved from the server database (either 10, 20 or as specified (via the *Other* option). The *Default* option effectively switches off the partial results option.

There follows a recap on Section 5.1. End users are able to create and maintain database queries and store their results in their PCs. Queries can be re-run at any time, overwriting (refreshing) any previously obtained results from the same query. Queries can be changed, or copied and changed, to produce new queries.

End users will have been provided, by the designer, with one or more Universes. Each Universe will comprise a number of objects, arranged into classes for convenience. Possibly unknown to the end user, each object is essentially a piece of SQL; a building block which can be combined with others to form a complete SQL statement, or query. When the query is run, the SQL statement is sent across to the server database and executed there, bringing the results back to the PC as a set of rows and columns which are stored on the PC's disk. Whenever the query is rerun, the results in the PC are overwritten or refreshed.

Queries are created and maintained through the use of a query builder screen into which objects, representing select items and conditional statements, are placed. Underlying database tables, and their relationships with one another, are built into these objects and are thus transparent to users of the query builder.

5.2 Reports

There are essentially three ways, or *templates*, in which data can be presented in reports:

> Tables
> Crosstabs (matrices)
> Charts

Each can be restructured into *master/detail* format.

A report can contain *s*everal alternative formats for the same query results. Each is contained within its own frame or *block* in the report, much like the frames of desktop publishing pages. These *data frames* can be accompanied by non-data frames containing presentational text and pictures. An example is shown below.

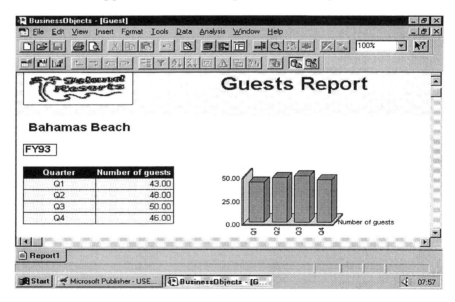

Reports are contained within *documents*, each document corresponding to a physical computer file. Several reports can be contained within the same document and printed out separately if required. A report can span across several document pages, although each individual report will start on a new page.

A report template can be converted to any other template and each can be converted to *master/detail* format and back again into normal format. The data from one data block can be copied into a new block before being converted.

Tables are simply the rows and columns of the data source (or *data provider* in Business Objects terms) which can be either the results of a query or the rows and columns of a local data file.

country	city	hotel	revenue	guests
UK	Leeds	Hilton	4,032.00	430
UK	Leeds	Ramada	2,104.00	212
UK	Manchester	Hilton	920.00	345
US	York	Marriot	4,210.00	144
US	York	National	2,010.00	411
US	York	Ramada	3,510.00	1322

In *crosstabs*, columns are selected to be the horizontal and vertical attributes, and internal values of, matrix representations.

	Hilton	Marriot	National	Ramada	Sum
Leeds	4,032.00			2,104.00	6,136.00
Manchester	920.00				920.00
York		4,210.00	2,010.00	3,510.00	9,730.00
	4,952.00	4,210.00	2,010.00	5,614.00	16,786.00

Charts are graphical representations of data such as histograms and pie charts.

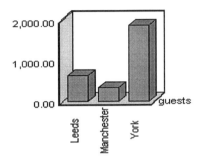

In [*multi-*]*master/detail* format, one [or more] columns are declared as *master* columns whose distinct values are separated out and used as headers to partition the sections into which the remaining columns, in the form of tables, crosstabs or charts, are segmented.

Each of the three templates, in either master/detail or normal format, are created with the aid of the *reports wizard*.

Note that many of the operations described in this chapter can be carried out within the *Slice and Dice* tool, described in Chapter 6.

If the *Report* toolbar is not currently in view, it can be obtained by moving the mouse pointer over the standard toolbar, pressing the

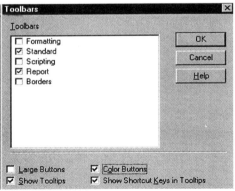  right mouse button and selecting the *Report* option from the pop-up menu (shown right). An alternative is to select the *Toolbars* option from the *View* menu and tick the *Reports* box in the pop-up window presented (shown left).

The way the toolbar is obtained is typical of the Business Objects User module in that there are often two or more different ways of achieving the same thing.

All new reports are created via the *Reports wizard*. The wizard can be invoked in several ways:

The wizard is automatically invoked when the Business Objects User module is first invoked. Be aware that if the wizard is not cancelled (by activating the *Cancel* button), a new report within a new document will be created.

The button shown on the right can be used at any time during the session to create a new report within a new document and invoke the wizard.

Selecting either the *table, crosstab* or *chart* option of the *Insert* menu option will create a new frame within the current report, and invoke the wizard. On selecting *table, crosstab* or *chart*, the mouse pointer symbol  will change and will need to be moved into a suitable location within the report and the left mouse button clicked.

Note that the individual reports within the currently opened document are represented as *tabs* at the bottom of the screen. A new blank report can be opened within the current document by selecting the *Report* option of the *Insert* menu option.

5.2.1 Creating Tables

New tables, like new crosstabs and charts, are created via the Reports wizard. The following screen will be presented when the wizard is invoked.

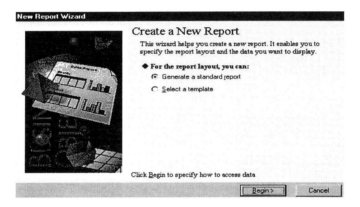

Because the first option (*Generate a standard report*) is available within the scope of the second option (*Select a template*), it can be ignored here. Selecting the second option and pressing the *Begin* button presents a list of templates as shown below.

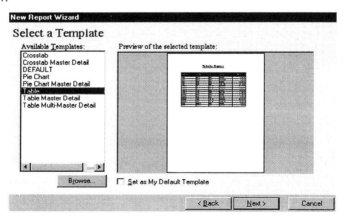

The three templates are included, plus their *master/detail* versions (and *master/master/detail* version in the case of tables). Selecting *Table* and pressing the *Next* button will reveal the *data providers* panel below which will always appear next, whatever template was selected. This panel asks from where the source data is to be taken, the two main options being a Universe (in which case the data will be the results of a query) or a local data file.

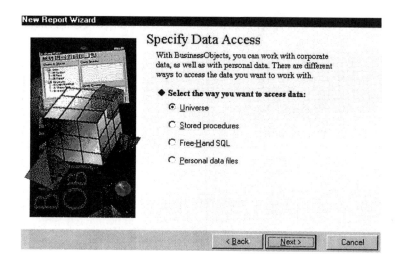

Having selected a data provider, the reports wizard will begin to do its work. The result is shown overleaf in which the columns and rows of the source data (query results or local data file) are simply restated, with the horizontal arrangement of columns and vertical ordering of rows unchanged. A simple report title is provided which can be altered as required (the ways in which reports can be altered in appearance are discussed in Chapter 7).

Tabular Report

country	city	hotel	revenue	guests
UK	Leeds	Hilton	4,032.00	430
UK	Leeds	Ramada	2,104.00	212
UK	Manchester	Hilton	920.00	345
US	Chicago	Marriot	4,210.00	144
US	Dallas	National	2,010.00	411
US	Dallas	Ramada	3,510.00	1322

5.2.2 Creating Crosstabs

On page 76 it was stated that there are three ways to invoke the reports wizard. If the third way is used (i.e. selecting *Crosstab* from the *Insert* menu option), the wizard will prompt for additional information, as shown below.

On selecting one of the three options, the wizard will present the panel above.

If the top option is selected and the *Begin* button used, the panel shown below
will be presented showing all the *dimension* and *measure* objects of the data source.

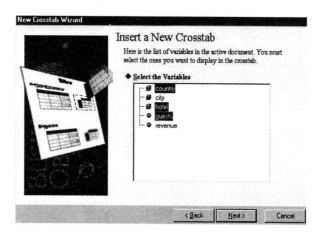

Having selected the objects required and activated the *Next* button, the panel
below will be presented through which the user will be able to declare which objects
are to be the horizontal and which the vertical ones of the crosstab.

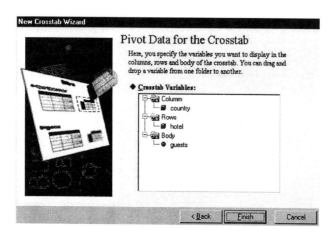

The process of rearranging columns is referred to in Business Objects terms as *pivoting*. Objects can be dragged from one axis to the other as necessary and the Finish button pressed to produce the crosstab block, shown below.

	Hilton	Marriot	National	Ramada
UK	775.00			212.00
US		144.00	411.00	1,322.00

Note that the crosstab above could have been inserted into a new report within the current document by selecting the *Report* option of the *Insert* menu. The new report will be indicated by the appearance of a new report tab at the foot of the screen. On the other hand, the crosstab could have been inserted into an existing report in which case it will appear alongside other templates that already exist in the report (table, crosstab or chart). Bear in mind, however, that if the new crosstab is not particularly related to other templates in the same report, it ought to be placed into another report, or even in another document altogether. And if it *is* related to another template, the two templates ought to be *linked* together by common keys. In this way the two templates (e.g. a table and chart) will "run in parallel" and any sectionalization (i.e. in master/detail reports) will be applied to both templates, as shown in the example below.

FY93

Quarter	Number of guests
Q1	43.00
Q2	48.00
Q3	50.00
Q4	46.00

5.2.3 Creating Charts

Using the *Insert* menu option *Chart*, the panel below will be presented.

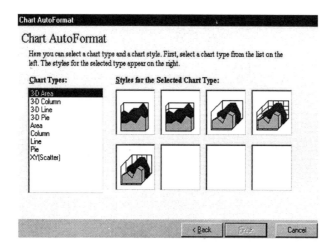

Selecting an option will produce the finished product, an example of which is shown below.

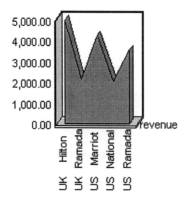

5.2.4 Pivoting

Whatever is seen in the tables, crosstabs and charts of a report, bear in mind that the *whole of* the source data (e.g. query results) will always be available in memory "behind the report". This section describes how rows and columns can be rapidly switched between background memory and report and how columns can be rearranged horizontally and rows reordered vertically.

The removing and rearranging of columns are described in Business Objects terms as *pivoting*. Rows are reordered and removed through the use of processes described in Business Objects terms as *sorting* and *filtering,* respectively.

The pivoting menus can be obtained by clicking anywhere in the table, crosstab or chart and selecting the *Table, Crosstab* or *Chart* option, respectively, from the *Format* menu. The pivoting panels will differ between table, crosstab and chart.

The pivoting panel for the table template is shown overleaf and is one of five tabs, the other four of which will be described later on. In the left window are all the columns of the source data, presented as objects. In the right window are those currently included in the table, in the order in which they appear. For tables, the *Columns* and *Rows* folders can be ignored. Objects can be removed from the table by clicking on the object (in the right window) and activating the *Remove* button. Previously removed columns can be reinstated by clicking on the object (in the left window) and activating the *Add* button. The ordering of columns (left to right) in the table can be changed by clicking on an object (in the right window) and using the *Move Up* and *Move Down* buttons to move the column to the left or to the right, respectively, of the column next to it.

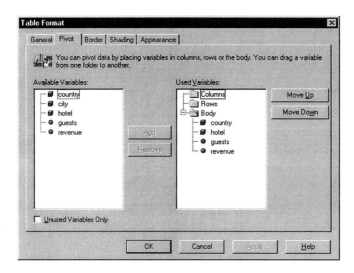

In the case of crosstabs, there will be *dimension* objects under the rows and column folders and *measure* objects within the body folder.

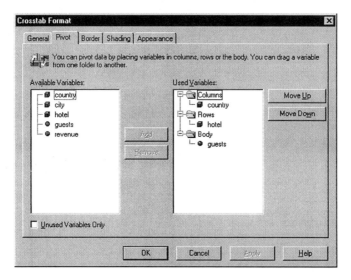

The panel at the bottom of the previous page corresponds to the crosstab at the top of page 81. Moving and swapping objects around as shown in the panel below will change the crosstab as shown below that: *country* has been removed, *city* brought under the *rows* folder, *hotel* moved from the rows to the *columns* folder and *guests* replaced by *revenue* in the the report body.

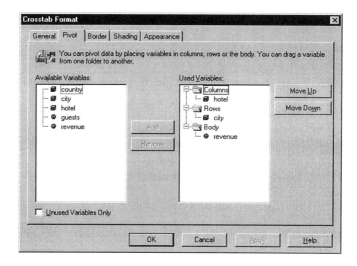

	Chicago	Dallas	Leeds	Manchester
Hilton			4,032.00	920.00
Marriot	4,210.00			
National		2,010.00		
Ramada		3,510.00	2,104.00	

The pivot panel for charts is slightly different in that the right hand window has folders for X, Y and Z axes instead of columns, rows and body. The principle for rearranging charts is the same: removing, adding and switching between axes. The example below involves swapping *revenue* for *guests,* removing *country* from the X axis and adding *city* to the Z axis. Note that using the (formally unused) Z axis will make the chart into a three-dimensional one.

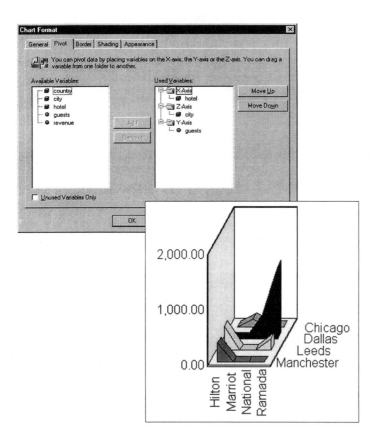

5.2.5 Filtering

Filtering is the process of preventing certain source data records from being carried into a table crosstab or chart. These record removals are "temporary" in that records can be reinstated (from memory) just as quickly as they are removed. The criteria for removal is expressed in terms of column values and is applied by clicking anywhere in the table, crosstab or chart and selecting the *Filters* option of the *Format* menu. The panel shown below appears.

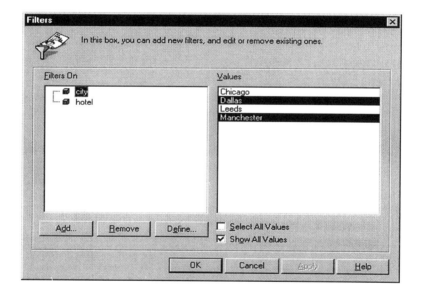

The left window of the panel informs the user that two columns are currently being filtered (*city* and *hotel*). The right window shows a list of all the distinct values of the column currently highlighted in the left window, of which only those highlighted are being carried into the table (i.e. all source data rows associated with Leeds and Chicago are being ignored, or *filtered out*). A filter is removed by

highlighting its column in the left window and using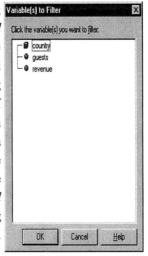
the *Remove* button. Filters are created by using the *Add*
button, which will open up the panel shown on the
right. The objects presented will be all those included
in the table, crosstab or chart that are not already being
filtered. One or more can be highlighted and the *OK*
button pressed. Returning to the main Filters panel on
the previous page, the *Select All Values* tick-box is a
quick way of highlighting *all* the distinct values of the
right window; useful when only one or two of a large
number of values need to be filtered out. The *Show All*
Values tick-box stops unhighlighted values from being
displayed in the right window, for convenience (i.e.
reducing the list to Dallas and Manchester only).

The *Define* button opens up this somewhat simplistic approach to filtering into
the more comprehensive way of applying *record selection criteria*. The panel
shown below is opened up in which full blown expressions can be built up,
incorporating several columns.

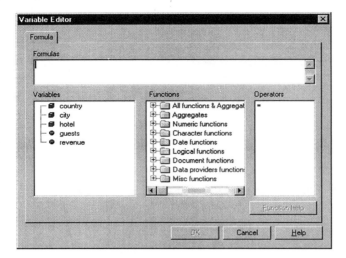

The before-filtering and after-filtering versions of the table shown on page 79 are shown below:

city	country	guests	revenue
Chicago	US	144.00	4,210.00
Dallas	US	1,733.00	5,520.00
Leeds	UK	642.00	6,136.00
Manchester	UK	345.00	920.00

city	country	guests	revenue
Dallas	US	1,733.00	5,520.00
Manchester	UK	345.00	920.00

An alternative to using the *Filters* option of the Format menu is to use the filter button, shown right. This is used on a column-by-column basis because a column needs to be highlighted first in the table, crosstab or chart. The window presented by the Filter button is similar to the right window of the Filters panel shown on page 87. As soon as the column is clicked, the button will indicate whether a filter exists or not for that column by being depressed or not, respectively. If a depressed button is clicked, the filter will be removed, so to *change* a column's filter it is advisable to use the *Filters* option of the *Format* menu.

5.2.6 Sorting

The rows of a table or crosstab can be ordered, or *sorted*, by using the sort  buttons, shown left. The left button sorts ascendingly, the right one descendingly. Like filters, sorts are applied on a column-by-column basis. For example, clicking on a *country* column of a table or crosstab and then clicking on the left sort button will rearrange the rows of the table or crosstab in ascending order of countries. Clicking on *city* and then clicking on the right sort button will rearrange the rows in descending order of city within ascending order of country (since the country sort will still be in place). If the country column is now clicked again and the (now depressed) left sort button pressed (to remove the sort), the rows of the table or crosstab will be arranged into descending order of cities only.

5.2.7 Master/Detail

Tables, crosstabs and charts can all be restructured on a *master/detail* basis. This requires only that one of the columns (dimension objects) of the table, crosstab or chart be declared the *master* column; the reports wizard will do the rest.

A table can be restructured into master/detail format by selecting one of its dimension objects, by clicking on the column heading or below it, and either (a) clicking the *Set as Master* button (shown right), (b) clicking the right mouse button and selecting the *Set as Master* option from it or (c) selecting the *Set as Master* option from the *Format* menu option.

The reports wizard will restructure the table and produce the result shown below.

Tabular Report

UK

hotel	revenue	guests
Hilton	4,952.00	775.00
Ramada	2,104.00	212.00

US

hotel	revenue	guests
Marriot	4,210.00	144.00
National	2,010.00	411.00
Ramada	3,510.00	1,322.00

Crosstabs can be restructured into master/detail format in the same way.

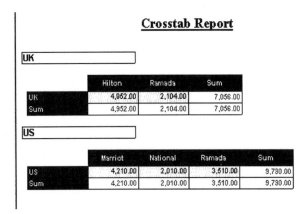

Restructuring a chart into master/detail format can only be achieved by converting a master/detailed table or crosstab into a chart or using the *Slice and Dice* tool (described in Section 6.1).

A second master column can be specified in the same way as the first, by highlighting the column and activating the *Set to Master* button. An example is shown below where the table shown on page 91 has been sectionalized by hotel.

Tabular Report

UK

Hilton

revenue	guests
4,952.00	775.00

Ramada

revenue	guests
2,104.00	212.00

Master/detail formatting can be removed by clicking anywhere in the table block, selecting the *Apply Template* from the *Format* menu option and selecting *Table, Crosstab* or *Chart* from the list.

Changing the column declared as the master can be achieved by either selecting *Undo* from the *Edit* menu option (if *Set to Master* was the last operation performed) or removing the master/detail formatting altogether (as described above) and starting again. The proper way to do it, however, can be explained by introducing the concept of report *sections*.

5.2.8 Sections

Whenever a report is structured into *master/detail* format, it is *sectionalized,* one section per master column. Thus, the table shown on page 92 will have two sections associated with countries and hotels, respectively, the latter being *inside* the former. Changing the master column is achieved by first highlighting the section we are interested in and then invoking the *section editor*. A section is highlighted by clicking away from the table block (to clear the highlighting process) and then clicking next to a master column. For example, highlighting the countries section can be achieved by clicking next to any of the countries master columns (when all will be highlighted).

Once highlighted, sections are indicated by labelled horizontal lines. For example, clicking next to (but not inside) the UK master column of the table block shown on page 92 will reveal the view shown top left overleaf. Clicking next to the Hilton column will reveal the view shown below and to the right of it.

Sections are also discussed on page 100.

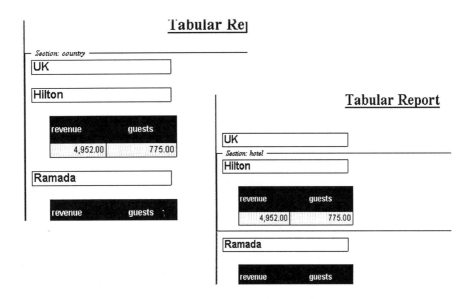

The section editor can now be invoked by selecting the *Section* option of the *Format* menu option. This will reveal the panel below.

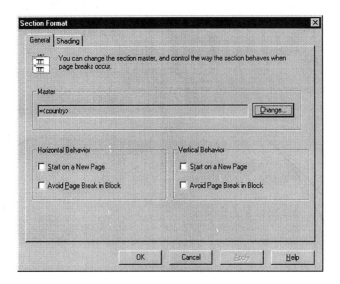

5.2.9 Breaks

Applying what Business Objects refers to as a *break* in a table or crosstab has almost the same effect as restructuring the table or crosstab into master/detail format. In master/detail arrangements, the master column is separated out and appears alone between the now separated *sections* into which the rest of the table or crosstab is subdivided. When a *break* is applied, on the other hand, the table or crosstab is also subdivided into sections at each change of value of the column to which the break was applied. However, this column remains with the table or crosstab.

A break is applied by clicking on a column in the table or crosstab and then clicking on the *Break* button, shown right. The result, shown below, can be compared with the equivalent Master/detail structure shown at the bottom of page 92.

country	hotel	revenue	guests
UK	Hilton	4,952.00	775.00
	Ramada	2,104.00	212.00
UK			

country	hotel	revenue	guests
US	Marriot	4,210.00	144.00
	National	2,010.00	411.00
	Ramada	3,510.00	1,322.00
US			

Typically, the break facility can be taken further by opening up the *Breaks editor panel*, obtained by clicking anywhere in the table or crosstab and selecting the *Breaks* option of the *Format* menu. The panel is shown overleaf.

The various options are explained as follows.

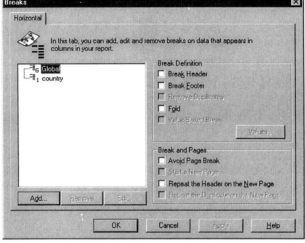

Break header	Inserts a header row at the top of each section of the broken table/crosstab (default).
Break footer	Inserts a footer row at the bottom of each section of the broken table/crosstab (default). A calculation can be placed into the footer (see page 98).
Remove duplicates	Removes all but one of every set of rows whose column values are all identical.
Fold	Removes all but the header and footer of each section of the table/crosstab.
Value-based break	Certain values of the break-column(s) can be declared to be conditionally ignored by the break process (i.e. any change of column values to these values will not be entertained by the break process.

New columns can be brought into the break process and existing ones removed using the *Add* and *Remove* buttons, respectively. The *Edit* button allows the columns declared as break columns to be reordered (i.e. their *break levels* to be changed).

The tick-boxes at the lower right of the *Breaks* panel are for controlling page breaks and include the following:

Start/avoid a new page	For a change of value of the specified column, a new page will be started/avoided.
Repeat the header on a new page	Header rows are repeated at the top of every new page.
Repeat the duplicate on the new page	Despite duplicates being suppressed, they will be restated (once only) at the top of each new page.

5.2.10 Calculations

Having applied *breaks* to reports, or restructured them into master/detail format, it is natural to apply break-level sub totals. These can be applied by clicking on a column value (or column header) and clicking on the *Insert Calculation* button, shown right. This opens up the panel shown below from which a variety of calculation types can be selected. An example is shown below.

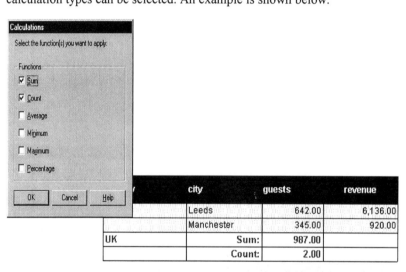

country	city	guests	revenue
	Leeds	642.00	6,136.00
	Manchester	345.00	920.00
UK	Sum:	987.00	
	Count:	2.00	

country	city	guests	revenue
US	Chicago	144.00	4,210.00
	Dallas	1,733.00	5,520.00
US	Sum:	1,877.00	
	Count:	2.00	

5.2.11 Ranking

Ranking is the process of presenting only the top n (or bottom n) records. For example, a sales manager might only want to look at the top 10 best selling products. Ranking is achieved by selecting a column (which must be a *dimension*) and using the *Apply Ranking* button (shown right). The panel shown below is opened up.

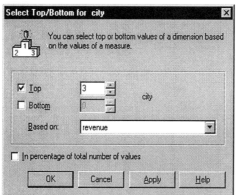

The top x and/or bottom y values can be specified together with a measure object on whose values the ranking is to be based. Note that where values of the dimension column are duplicated, the aggregate values will automatically be calculated.

The "before and after" results of the above specifications are shown below:

city	revenue
Chicago	555.00
Lisbon	554.00
London	3,554.00
Milan	12,343.00
New York	2,104.00
Nice	8,776.00
Paris	4,577.00
Rome	311.00

city	revenue
Milan	12,343.00
Nice	8,776.00
Paris	4,577.00

5.2.12 Folding

A table, crosstab or chart which has been structured in master/detail format may have a substantial number of sections; the same number as there are master columns. *Folding* means "hiding" part of the report. It is applied at section level and hides all information below the section at which it is applied. Folding is activated via the *section level buttons* obtained by selecting the *Outline* option of the *View* menu. For a table with two master columns, there will be two section-level buttons (labelled 1 and 2) and a report-wide level (labelled S).

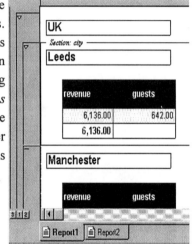

5.2.13 Converting from One Report Template to Another

A table or crosstab can be converted into a chart by clicking on it and selecting the *Turn to Chart* option of the *Format* menu. A chart can be converted into a table by clicking on it and selecting the *Turn to Table* option of the *Format* menu.

The *Apply Template* option of the *Format* menu can be used to convert a table into a crosstab, a crosstab into a table or a chart into a crosstab.

User Tools - Slice & Dice and Drill-Down

T he Slice & Dice tool enables the rows and columns of data, brought back to the PC by a database query, to be rearranged locally. The Drill-Down tool enables localized sections of the data brought back to the PC, by a database query, to be broken down into greater detail.

6.1 Slice and Dice

The action of adding and removing objects from reports (*pivoting*) and of specifying and changing master detail objects have thus far been carried out via the panels invoked from options of the *Format* menu. The *Slice & Dice* tool enables these activities to be carried out in a more intuitive way through the use of a single multi purpose panel, much like the query builder panel described in section 5.1, rendering all these activities to simple *drag and drop* operations.

Bear in mind that in snowflake structures, such as that illustrated below right, there could be considerable numbers of columns (or *keys*) suitable as candidates for Dimension objects - many of which could also serve as master ones in master/detail reports.

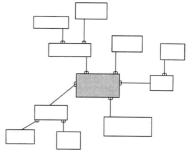

For example, Dimension objects could be selected from all ten tables in the diagram, or from just one or two. For master/detail reports, there are ten immediately obvious candidates for master objects and if you consider that some of the tables might contain their own internal hierarchies, there will be many more.

With such a complicated data model, the business of swapping and changing objects, as alternative report formats are investigated, would be a daunting one.

The *Slice & Dice* tool is invoked by clicking anywhere in an existing table, crosstab or chart and using the button shown right.

The main Slice & Dice screen is shown below and comprises three windows. On the left are all the objects available in the source data (query results or local flat file). These objects can be selected to act as either *Master* objects (by dragging them into the *Section* window at top right of the screen) or as objects in the main body of the table, crosstab or chart (by dragging them into the *Block Structure* window at bottom right of the screen).

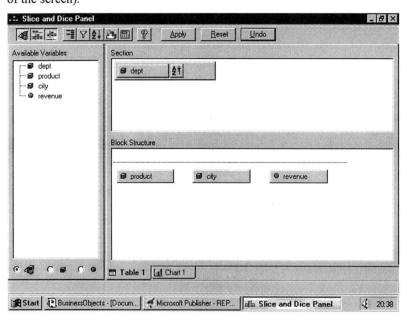

The three buttons in the bottom left of the screen allow the objects displayed in the window above to be restricted to Dimension objects only, Measure objects only or both. The three buttons at top left are, from left to right, to add/remove the available objects window, to add/remove the *section* window and to add/remove the status bar (along the bottom of the screen).

To the right of these buttons are our old friends the *Break*, *Filter*, *Sort*, *Ranking* and *Calculation* buttons (described on pages 87 through 99). The three buttons to the right of the *Help* button are, from left to right, to re-generate the report (upon which the Slice & Dice tool is directed), ditto but remove all formatting applied to the report (formatting is discussed in chapter 7) and to cancel all the actions performed since the last activation of any of the *Apply, Reset* and *Undo* buttons.

Where two or more report templates are present in the same report, there will be a tab for each along the bottom of the screen.

Objects may be *dragged* from any of the three windows into any other window (by holding down the left mouse button). *Sorts*, *Calculations* etc can be applied to objects in the *Section* and *Block Structure* window by clicking on the object to highlight it (the highlighting being indicated by the appearance of a back panel around the object's icon) and clicking on one of the five tool buttons (the *Sort*, *Calculation* etc icon will appear, and remain, below the object's icon.

An object in the *Section* window can be swapped with one in the *Block Structure* window, and vice versa, by holding down the *shift* key and dragging the first object over the second.

Note that there can be two or more objects (*Master* objects) in the *Section* window and these will be arranged vertically to indicate their hierarchical relationships.

To view the results of any actions (after activating the *Apply* or *Reset* buttons) the *Slice and Dice* panel will need to be minimised to reveal them behind.

Note that the action of dragging one or more of the objects in the *Block Structure* window above the broken line effectively converts a table into a crosstab (matrix) or a chart into a 3D chart. An example is shown below in which the *product* object has been moved above the line. The resulting report, shown at the bottom of the page, will be a master/detail report in which a crosstab, based on dimension objects *product* and *city*, will be arranged within master object *dept*.

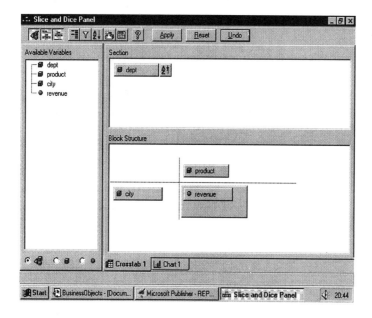

leisure		
	jackets	shirts
Chicago	12,332.00	54,332.00
Dallas	33,111.00	34,561.00
Texas	12,417.00	12,441.00

Note how the master object *dept* includes a *sort* icon. This was applied automatically by the system when the *dept* object was dragged into the *Section* window. *Sorts*, and any of its companions (*breaks*, *filters*, *rankings* and *calculations*), can be applied to the objects in the *Section* or *Block Structure* panels. In the example below a *sort* (descending) has been applied to *product*, a *filter* and *break* to *city* and a *calculation* (sum) to revenue. The resulting report is shown below the panel.

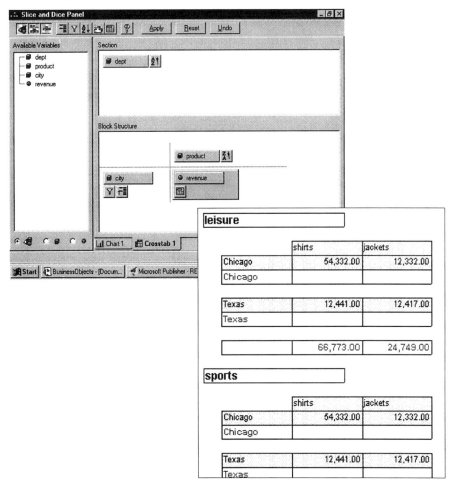

A table or crosstab can be converted into a chart, or a chart into a table, by clicking on the tab at the bottom of the screen, clicking the *right* mouse button and selecting the *Turn to chart* or *Turn to table* option from the pop-up menu. Other options in the pop-up menu are for removing and renaming the table, crosstab or chart.

A quick way of temporarily suppressing the master/detail nature of a report, without actually dragging the master object out of the Section window, is to use the *deactivate/reactivate* feature. This is achieved by clicking on a master object and clicking the *right* mouse button. This opens up the pop-up menu shown below. Selecting the *Deactivate* option will produce the results shown below. Note how *revenue* has been reaggregated in the absence of *dept*.

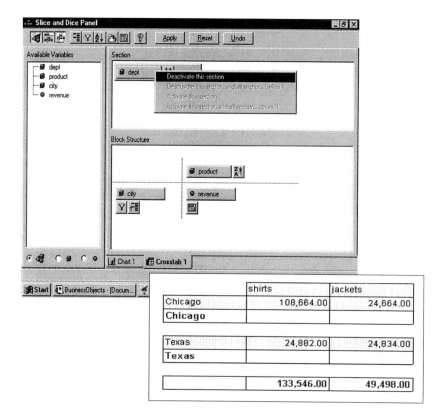

The *deactivate/reactivate* feature illustrates the rapid nature of the Slice & Dice tool which can thus be used to analyze data prior to getting down to the task of formatting reports (formatting is described in Chapter 7).

The Slice & Dice tool enables the rows and columns of data, brought back to the PC by database queries, to be rearranged locally. This activity is made easy through simple drag-and-drop actions, and includes the ability to switch around or remove column attributes, reorder rows, apply row filtering (record selection criteria) and freely swap around column attributes into matrix arrangements. The process of applying the changes is rapid since all the data is held within the PC's memory.

The Slice & Dice tool is thus a powerful one and can be used in conjunction with database queries in order to analyze rapidly, and in more detail, the "first cut" data extracts brought back from remote databases.

6.2 Drill-Down

What has become popularly known as *drill-down* is the process of delving deeper and deeper into a localized section of a hierarchically structured aggregate table in order to obtain finer and finer detail. For example, suppose a table comprises one *dimension* object (state) and one *measure* object (sales totals), and suppose it is observed that the sales for a particular state are somewhat lower than the general average among the other states. Using the Drill-Down tool, the user is able to break down the figures for that particular state into the next level of detail, say, *city*. Again, any city's figures which are unusually low can be further broken down into *store,* for example.

With a conventional break report the user could display either a *state*-level summary, a *city within state*-level summary or the sales figures for every store of every city of every state, but nothing in between. The Drill-Down tool enables a limited break-report to be produced in which breakdowns can be localized to particular areas of interest.

Although the *Slice and Dice* tool could, in theory, be used to home in on exceptional figures, the switching around of filters and objects would be hopelessly cumbersome.

The Drill-Down tool can only be applied to a table whose *dimension* objects are from a single class, or single *hierarchy*. Objects within classes must be hierarchically related to one another in the order in which they are arranged within the class. *Hierarchies* are described in Section 3.3 (page 18) and Section 4.2.7 (page 52), and are created by Business Objects Designers whenever objects from two or more classes need to be combined and arranged hierarchically for the specific benefit of Drill-Down users.

Note that a snowflake structure, like the one illustrated below, can contain numerous hierarchies, and that a given object can be a member of more than one of them. For example, given that the *dimension* objects of the various tables are labelled **a, b, c** and so on, the following are just a few of the possible hierarchies which could be identified within the data model:

a,c,d   b,c,d   a,e   e,a   n,m,a   e,a,d

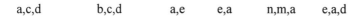
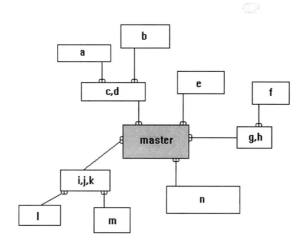

Note that the Drill-Down tool is only applicable to tables (as opposed to crosstabs and charts) and can only be used with tables produced by queries for which a *Scope of Analysis* has been specified (see Section 5.1.3 page 65). Such tables will look like any other tables, but will contain "hidden" dimension objects. The Drill-Down tool is invoked via the button shown above right.

As an example, in the table below, the revenue for the city of Texas is on the low side and thus is a prime candidate for drilling. This can be done in two ways:

city	revenue
Chicago	133,328.00
Dallas	135,344.00
Texas	53,716.00

(a)   Double-clicking the *dimension* cell *Texas* will take Texas out of the table and into a *master* object, and bring the next object in the hierarchy (let's say *Product*) into the table instead (i.e. all products within Texas).

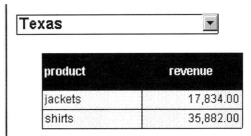

product	revenue
jackets	17,834.00
shirts	35,882.00

(b)   Double-clicking the *Measure* cell (i.e. the Texas revenue figure of
        53,716.00) will also take "Texas" out of the table and into a *master* object,
        but will bring into the table *all* the objects lower down in the current
        hierarchy. For example, were City a member of the following hierarchy:

                    City, Product, sales person,date

        the table below would result.

product	salesperson	date	revenue
jackets	FTS	Aug-96	12,417.00
jackets	PFD	May-96	5,417.00
shirts	ADR	July-96	12,441.00
shirts	RDC	July-96	23,441.00

        Having begun the Drill-down process, there are three alternatives for
proceeding:

(a)   The pick-list button at the right side of the master cell can be used to swap
        the master cell value from Texas for any other city value, the table contents
        being changed in response.

(b)   Whether the master cell value has been changed or not, the drill-down
        process can be reversed (i.e. Drill-Up); the data being reaggregated on the
        master object and the latter taken back into the body of the table.

(c)   The third option is to drill *across* to another hierarchy (or rather to the top
        level of another hierarchy) and start to drill-down from there. This is
        achieved by clicking the right mouse button anywhere in the table and
        selecting *Explore by* from the pop-up menu. A second pop-up menu will

result in which will be listed the next dimension object of the "current" hierarchy (unless the bottom of the hierarchy has been reached) and the top dimension objects of each of any other hierarchies will beavailable.

There follows a brief recap on the manipulation of tables and crosstabs:

On the face of it, a table is nothing more than a replica of raw query results. Tables are an obvious way of presenting "lists"; that is, rows of essentially non numerical information (*dimension* and *detail* objects), ordered as required. Tables are also the way to present break reports; that is, keys and values (i.e. *dimension* objects and *measure* objects), hierarchically ordered with subtotals at key value breakpoints and with repeating key values suppressed. The Business Objects' *Break* facility is the most straight forward way to produce break reports. The alternative *master/detail* facility will need to be used, however, when it is required to present tables and charts alongside one another in the same report (see page 81).

Crosstabs are matrices in which distinct values of two *dimension* objects are arranged horizontally and vertically (in rows and columns) with the aggregated values of *measure* objects arranged at intersection points (i.e. of the row and column corresponding to the *dimension* objects on which they are based).

If a crosstab needs to be segmented according to a third (or fourth) dimension object, it is better to use the *master/detail* Business Objects facility (rather than the *Break* facility) which will separate the *master dimension* objects out of the crosstab and use them as headers between separate crosstabs.

CHAPTER 7

User Tools - Fine Tuning the Appearance of Reports

The tables and crosstabs of reports are created by the Reports Wizard and subsequently modified, if necessary, through the use of the various tools described in Chapters 5 and 6. Although the final results are perfectly presentable, there is nonetheless a comprehensive range of reformatting facilities that can be applied to change the *appearance*, rather than the data content, of reports. This chapter describes these facilities and it does so "by example" in which the appearance of a table is progressively altered through the application of a series of reformatting steps.

The first example shows how the table shown below can be reformatted into the break report shown overleaf, by applying the step-by-step instructions that follow.

country	city	hotel	revenue
UK	Leeds	Hilton	4,032.00
UK	Leeds	Ramada	2,104.00
UK	Manchester	Hilton	920.00
US	Chicago	Marriot	4,210.00
US	Dallas	National	2,010.00
US	Dallas	Ramada	3,510.00

UK	Leeds	Hilton	£4,032.00
		Ramada	£2,104.00
	Leeds total		**£6,136.00**
	Manchester	Hilton	£920.00
	Manchester total		**£920.00**
UK total			**£7,056.00**
US	Chicago	Marriot	£4,210.00
	Chicago total		**£4,210.00**
	Dallas	National	£2,010.00

To remove all grid lines, click on the top left cell ("Country") and, while holding down the shift key, click on the lower right cell ("3,510,000") of the table. Select *Cell* from the *Format* menu. This opens up the *Cell Format* panel. Select the *Border* tab, and in the *Border* panel (shown below) click the "None" box in the *Presets* area (top left of screen) then click on OK.

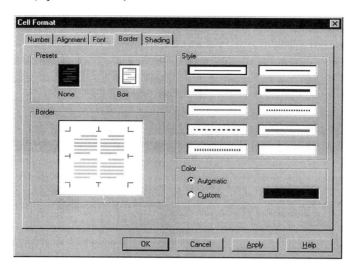

The result is shown below.

country	city	hotel	revenue
UK	Leeds	Hilton	4,032.00
UK	Leeds	Ramada	2,104.00
UK	Manchester	Hilton	920.00
US	Chicago	Marriot	4,210.00
US	Dallas	National	2,010.00
US	Dallas	Ramada	3,510.00

To get rid of the column headers, click on the top left cell ("Country") and, while holding down the shift key click on the top right cell ("revenue") of the table. Select *Delete* from the *Edit* menu.

To remove all color, click on the top left cell ("UK") and, while holding down the shift key, click on the lower right cell ("3,510,000") of the table. Select *Cell* from the *Format menu* and select the *Shading* tab.

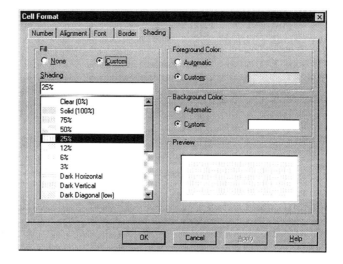

Move the slider (to the right of the Shading window) up to the top and click on the top option ("Clear (0%)"); then click on *OK*.

Now break the table on Country first, followed by city: that is, click on any *country* column and then click on the *Break* button (see page 95). Now click on any city column and on the *Break* button. The result is shown overleaf.

UK	Leeds	Hilton	4,032.00
		Ramada	2,104.00
	Leeds		
	Manchester	Hilton	920.00
	Manchester		
UK			

US	Chicago	Marriot	4,210.00
	Chicago		
	Dallas	National	2,010.00
		Ramada	3,510.00
	Dallas		
US			

Note that footers have been inserted automatically (by default) and are boxed. To remove the box, click on the left cell of the first bordered line. Note how all corresponding cells are highlighted throughout the table. While holding down the *shift* key, click on the right cell of the same lines (the *shift* key highlights all the cells between the one already highlighted and the one being clicked on now). Now hold down the *control* key and click on the left cell ("UK") of the remaining bordered line (the *control* key preserves the highlighting of all currently highlighted cells and adds to them the newly highlighted cell). Keep the *control* key depressed and click on the remaining three cells of the bordered line. Select *Cell* from the *Format menu*. Select the *Border* tab and, in the *Border* panel, click the "None" box in the *Presets* area (top left of screen) then click on *OK*.

Now add totals into the footer lines by clicking on any revenue figure and clicking on the *Calculation* button, ticking the *Sum* box in the Calculation panel (see page 98). The result is shown below.

UK	Leeds	Hilton	4,032.00
		Ramada	2,104.00
	Leeds	**Sum:**	**6,136.00**
	Manchester	Hilton	920.00
	Manchester	**Sum:**	**920.00**
UK		**Sum:**	**7,056.00**
US	Chicago	Marriot	4,210.00
	Chicago	**Sum:**	**4,210.00**
	Dallas	National	2,010.00
		Ramada	3,510.00
	Dallas	**Sum:**	**5,520.00**
US		**Sum:**	**9,730.00**

Now format all the figures to currency format by clicking on the top right figure ("4,032,000") and while holding down the *control* key, clicking on any city total (e.g. "6,136,000") and then any country total (e.g. "7,056,000"). Now select the *Cell* option of the *Format* menu and select the *Number* tab. In the Number panel (shown overleaf), select *Currency* from the pick-list in the left window and select the top option from the right window. Incidentally, were the figure in the table to have been the number of guests instead of revenue, the *Number* option of the left window together with the "0" option of the right window could be selected to get rid of the decimal point (i.e. converting the figure into an integer).

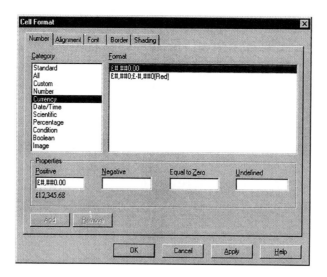

The next step is to get rid of all the "Sum:" text items. This is achieved by *double* clicking on the cell, pressing the space bar and then pressing the *return* key (this is done for each cell in turn).

Now insert a blank line after each total, for clarity. This is achieved by clicking on one of the total figures and then clicking on the *Add new cell below* button (shown left). Fortunately, this works for all totals.

The next task is to add some readability to the report by *double* clicking on any of the emboldened city cells (in the totals lines) and appending the text already in the cell, as shown below:

                    =<city>+" total"   Then press the *return* key.

Note that an alternative to double-clicking is to single-click the cell and then select the *Edit Formula* option of the *Format* menu. This opens up the *Formula Editor* panel (shown overleaf) in which can be found a whole range of text editing functionality.

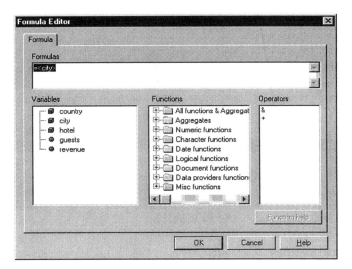

The last procedure can be repeated for the *country total* text item.

There is just one final task to perform which is to rectify the fact that there is not enough room for the "Manchester total" text string. On the face of it, this can be achieved by clicking on the cell to highlight it, moving the cursor to the right edge (where the pointer changes to two parallel vertical lines with outwardly pointing arrows), holding down the mouse button, and dragging the cell edge to the right a bit. The result of this however, is to move the revenue figure on the right out of position in relation to the other revenue figures above and below it.

To correct such an action, select the *Undo* option of the *Edit* menu. Now highlight the "Manchester total" cell again but also highlight all the other cells (see below) above and below the "Manchester total" cell, using the *control* key, whose lines include a revenue value (total or otherwise). The cell widths can now be dragged wider as described above (and will all move together this time).

UK	Leeds	Hilton	£4,032.00
		Ramada	£2,104.00
	Leeds total		**£6,136.00**
	Manchester	Hilton	£920.00
	Manchester tot		**£920.00**
UK total			**£7,056.00**
US	Chicago	Marriot	£4,210.00
	Chicago total		**£4,210.00**
	Dallas	National	£2,010.00

A second exercise will demonstrate a few other editing features. This involves converting a default table into a master/detail report; the before and after versions are illustrated below.

country	city	hotel	revenue
UK	Leeds	Hilton	4,032.00
UK	Leeds	Ramada	2,104.00
UK	Manchester	Hilton	920.00
US	Chicago	Marriot	4,210.00
US	Dallas	National	2,010.00
US	Dallas	Ramada	3,510.00

UK	Total currency is £		£7,056.00

city	hotel	revenue
Leeds	Hilton	£4,032.00
Leeds	Ramada	£2,104.00
Manchester	Hilton	£920.00

US	Total currency is £		£9,730.00

city	hotel	revenue
Chicago	Marriot	£4,210.00

The first step is to create a sum, which will by default be placed in a footer line. To do this, click on any of the revenue values and activate the *Calculation* button (see page 98). The result is shown below.

country	city	hotel	revenue
UK	Leeds	Hilton	4,032.00
UK	Leeds	Ramada	2,104.00
UK	Manchester	Hilton	920.00
US	Chicago	Marriot	4,210.00
US	Dallas	National	2,010.00
US	Dallas	Ramada	3,510.00
		Sum:	16,786.00

Now separate country out of the table as a master object by clicking on any country column and activating the *Set to Master* button (see page 91). The result is shown below.

UK		

city	hotel	revenue
Leeds	Hilton	4,032.00
Leeds	Ramada	2,104.00
Manchester	Hilton	920.00
	Sum:	7,056.00

US		

city	hotel	revenue
Chicago	Marriot	4,210.00

Now reduce the width of the Country cell by clicking in the cell, to highlight it, moving the cursor to its right edge, holding down the left mouse button and dragging the edge to the left. Now add two more cells to the right of this cell by highlighting the cell and activating the *Add to Right*  cell button (shown right). Now widen the new cell and, while it is highlighted, activate the *Add to Right* button again. The result is shown below.

UK		

city	hotel	revenue
Leeds	Hilton	4,032.00
Leeds	Ramada	2,104.00
Manchester	Hilton	920.00
	Sum:	7,056.00

US		

city	hotel	revenue

Now highlight the Sum value and, while holding down the shift key and the left mouse button, drag it into the rightmost of the new cells. Convert the value to currency, as described on page 121. Now double-click in the leftmost of the new cells and enter: "Total revenue is ". The three cells that make up the line from which the total revenue was dragged can be deleted by highlighting all of them and selecting *Delete* from the *Edit* menu.

CHAPTER 8

Data Mining

Data mining is the process of applying a variety of record selection criteria to a data set and searching amongst the resulting data subsets for those with significant characteristics. In business terms, the aim is to identify patterns and trends, or derive target groupings for marketing purposes. In technical terms, the aim is to identify subsets in which a particular value of a particular object is higher or lower than average. For example: "in a population of customers, what particular combinations of age group, gender and salary range result in sub groups whose members are big spenders or buy more shoes than shirts?".

Using the Slice & Dice and Drill-Down tools for such purposes would be cumbersome. In any case, Slice & Dice and Drill-Down are concerned with providing *Measure* object values associated with distinct sets of *Dimension* object values. Data mining, on the other hand, is concerned with the searching out of interesting data correlations that may lie hidden within a mass of data; or "mining for gold".

To further illustrate the mining technique, consider a data source whose records comprise attributes (objects) of gender, product, age, date and salary. The mining process involves selecting one of the available objects to be the *output object* and building a hierarchical *decision tree* using the remaining objects. For example, if salary range were selected to be the *output* object, remaining objects gender, product, age and date can be arranged into a decision tree. In our example, it just so happens that there is no natural hierarchical relationship between gender, product, age and date (i.e. the objects are interchangeable as parents and children). There are thus several possible decision tree structures involving the four objects.

A typical decision tree is shown below. Each of the boxes in the tree diagram are referred to as *nodes* and the source data becomes more and more filtered as it journeys downwards from node to node (n.b. the word *universe* is used here in its general sense and has no bearing upon Business Objects *Universes*).

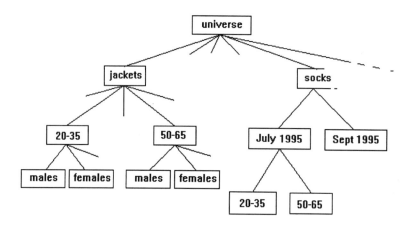

A restriction of the data mining tool is that all the "child" nodes emanating from a given "parent" node will be based upon the same object (i.e. each representing one or more of its distinct values (or value ranges if numeric). There is no restriction however on the choice of object on which to base child nodes i.e. two nodes sharing the same parent node can have child nodes based on different objects (as have nodes *jackets* and *socks* above).

Note that although there may be x number of distinct values of a given object in the source data (universe), there will usually be fewer numbers of distinct values of the same object in different nodes (that is, within different subsets of the source data). The number of distinct values of a given object at a given node, relative to the number for other objects at the same node, is referred to in Business Objects terms as the object's *discriminating power*.

The mining tool will always know the discriminating power of any object at any node and this is useful to the user when building up decision trees. In fact the mining tool can be delegated the task of building up an entire decision tree just by being supplied with a list of objects and the choice of *output* object. Alternatively, the mining tool can aid the user during the manual process of building up the tree by supplying the discriminating powers of objects at given nodes as the tree is built up node by node.

Decision trees can be large and complex. Consider for example the snowflake structure shown below in which many objects can take part in a mining exercise. The marketeer might not know which objects, nor which of their values, are likely to be significant (i.e. which might bring to light sub groups suitable for mail-shot targeting) but might have some intuition about certain objects and certain of their values. He or she can get the Mining tool to help out, but provide one or two intuitive leads along the way.

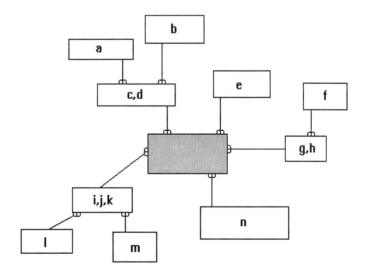

Each node represents a distinct subset of the source data and each will be associated with a particular set of conditions. For each node, the Business Objects Data Mining tool will produce two different kinds of results, depending on whether the node declared as the *output* object is numerical or non numerical.

For numerical output objects:

minimum, maximum, average and standard deviation, unless the user has specified value ranges (referred to in Business Objects terms as *thresholds*), in which case the results will be the same as for non numerical output objects.

For non numerical output objects:

the number of records associated with each distinct value of the object, together with the proportion they represent of the total number of records represented in the node.

The number of *child* nodes emanating from a given *parent* node can be reduced by instructing the mining tool to merge nodes. For example, the two age-group nodes (20-35 and 50-65) in the tree diagram shown on page 128 can be merged into a single node for which the two conditions would be 'OR-ed' together (i.e. the new node's condition would be "aged between 20 and 35 or aged between 50 and 65"). The mining tool can also be instructed to hide from view (or, in Business Objects terms, *fold*) nodes from the diagram making the diagram easier to read.

Users can also get the data mining tool to assign derived values to null-valued objects in the source data. The tool will randomly assign one or another of the distinct values found for the object in other non null-valued data source records, in proportion to the overall distribution of the distinct values within the source data set as a whole. This helps to keep sampling quantities as high as possible (but must be used with caution).

Bear in mind that decision trees can be quite large and complex, and difficult to analyse (or *mine*). Fortunately, a number of Business Objects tools are available to help out with the mining process:

- The user is able to get the computer to apply colour coding to nodes, based on their result ranges - making interesting nodes easier to spot..

- Using the *Discovering Rules* tool, the user specifies some desirable node results and the computer searches for them, displaying the record selection criteria (or in Business Objects terms *rules*) associated with any nodes it finds.

- The *What If* tool operates in reverse in that the user suggests some object value combinations (rules) and gets the computer to apply them and display the corresponding node results.

Either way, users are able to play around with their data sources - getting the computer to help them create alternative decision trees and to search them for gold.

The first stage in the use of the Business Objects Data Mining tool is to create a new *project* and this is achieved by clicking on the *New Project* button shown on the right. This invokes the New Project wizard, which presents the panel shown below.

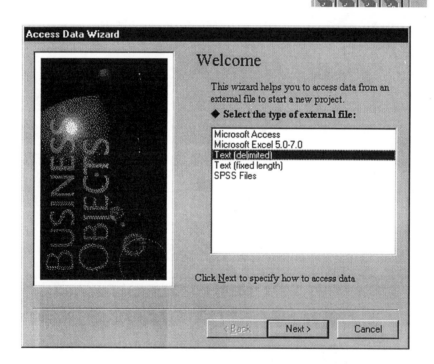

A number of data source options are presented. For demonstration purposes, a text file whose columns are separated by commas and whose first record contains column names is selected.

On activating the *Next* button, the panel shown below prompts for a data filename.

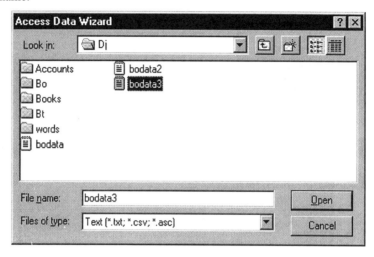

On double clicking a filename, the confirmation panel below will be presented.

On activating the *Next* button the panel below is presented, into which some
formatting specifications can be declared.

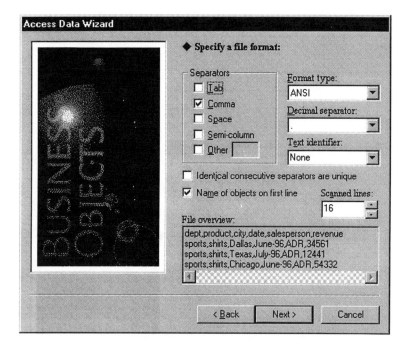

For our purposes here, the comma is declared as the column delimiter and the
tick-box checked to indicate that the first record contains column labels. Note how
the file's data content is displayed in the lower window.

The *Next* button invokes the panel shown overleaf in which are displayed the
objects (columns) and their data types. By default, all are scheduled to take part in
the mining exercise. Objects are eliminated from the exercise by clicking on the
object and changing the *yes* to *no*.

The next panel, shown overleaf, prompts for the object to be used as the
output object.

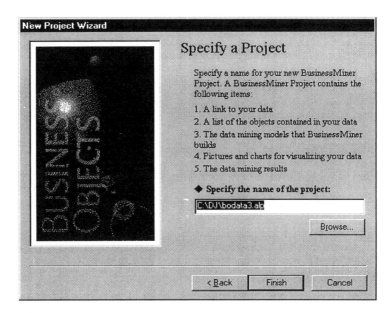

Note that at this point the wizard can be instructed, via the tick-box in the lower part of the panel, to continue on its own and create a complete decision tree. In doing this, the wizard will take into account a range of tree-building options. Default options are provided by Business Objects and can be changed by the user. If the user wishes to change them, the changes must be made before the automatic tree-building option is selected. These options are described later, together with a description of how the automatic tree-building process is carried out. In fact, there are varying degrees to which the building of the decision tree can be delegated to the wizard - either fully, not at all, or with control being passed to the wizard at any stage of a manual tree-building session.

Without opting for automatic tree-building, the next panel prompts for a data filename in which to store the project details.

Activating the *Finish* button completes the project building stage and the main project window (shown below) is presented, through which the tree-building process can begin.

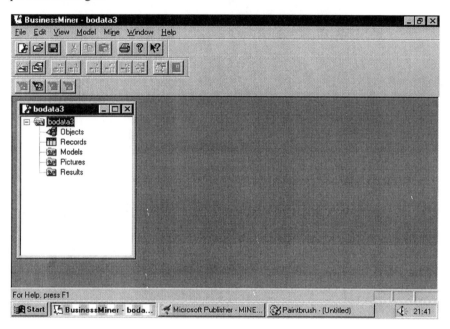

At this early stage of a project, only three window panes are available. The project pane is shown above, from which the *Objects* and *Records* panes can be obtained by double-clicking their icons. These window panes are shown overleaf.

The objects window panel is shown below and the results window below it.

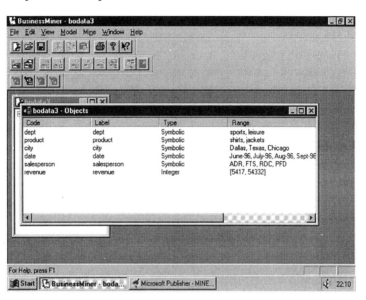

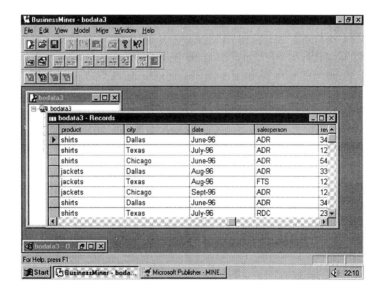

Now that once a project has been created, one or more decision trees (or *models* in Business Objects terms) can be created. As mentioned earlier, there are varying degrees to which the building of the decision tree can be delegated to the wizard, either fully, not at all, or with control being passed to the wizard at any stage of a manual tree-building session.

Each stage of the tree-building process is invoked via the *Model* menu option, invoking the pop-up menu shown right. When a new tree is being created (as now), there are just two tree-building options. These essentially offer a choice between automatic and manual tree-building:

Build Full Tree	Ctrl+T
Build Root Node	Ctrl+R
Expand Tree One Level	
Collapse Tree One Level	
Expand Selection	
Expand Selection One Level	
Expand Selection With...	
Expand Selection With Next	
Collapse Selection	Del
Group	
Ungroup	
Fold	-
Unfold	+
Rename Tree...	
Rename Node...	
Modify Building Options...	
Modify Display Options...	

Build Full Tree   which causes the wizard to create a complete tree, using the tree-building options currently set (these can be changed, before proceeding by selecting menu option *Modify Building Options*)

Build Root Node   which creates the first tree node (a single "universe" node, representing the complete and unfiltered source data)

Automatic tree-building is discussed later. The *Build Root Node* option will open up the *Tree* window shown overleaf. At the same time, a new *Tree* icon will appear under the *Model* folder in the main project window and its window pane opened up, as shown overleaf. Note that there are 12 records in the demo universe being used here and that the shirt/jacket ratio in the universe as a whole is 50/50.

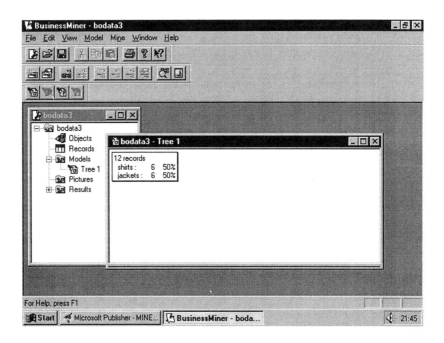

Now is a good time to look at the *display options*. These are obtained via option *Modify Display Options* of the *Model* menu (p 138). The resulting panel is shown overleaf. Note that all options are ticked; were *Object to Analyze* <u>not</u> ticked, no details at all of the object declared the *output* object would be displayed (only the number of records in the universe would be displayed). The *Leaves only* option will be discussed later. Because the *Sum* and *Proportion* boxes are ticked, the respective numbers and relative proportions of shirts and jackets displayed. Because the *Number of Records* box is ticked, the number of records in the node as a whole (the universe in this case) is displayed. The *Condition* box will be discussed later on. Finally, if the *Other Objects* box is ticked and one or more objects selected from the list, items other than products (the *output* object) can be caused to be displayed. At the bottom of page 140 are shown the results of some new display options.

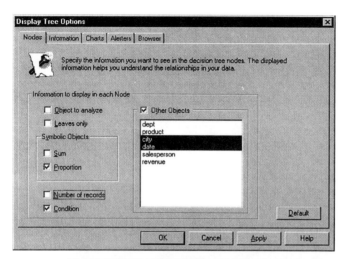

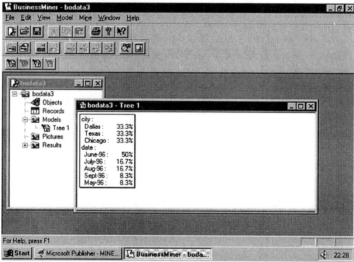

The next stage of the tree-building process is to create a new set of nodes off existing nodes, each the result of a filter based on a different value (or range of values if numeric) of a specified object.

The manual process of building up the decision tree can be helped by the Business Objects tool on a variety of fronts. Such help is obtained by adjusting (if necessary) the default settings in the panels of the *Modify Building Options* option of the *Model* menu and using the following building options of the *Model* menu:

> Expand Selection With
> Expand Selection One Level
> Expand Tree One Level
> Expand Selection with Next
> Expand Selection

8.1 Expand Selection With

This option allows the user to specify the object on which to base a new set of "child" nodes emanating from a highlighted node. Selecting the option will invoke the panel below.

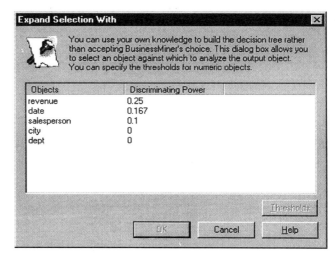

A pick-list of objects is presented and against each is shown its *discriminating power* (explained on page 128).

Double-clicking on date, for example, will create some new nodes, as shown below.

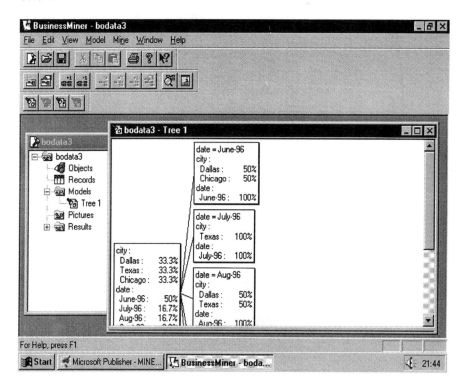

Note that a new node has been created for each distinct value of date. For widely ranging dates, the number of nodes could become unwieldy. Fortunately there is a way to reduce their numbers and this involves opening up the *Modify Building Options* panel, invoked via the *Model* menu. The panel is shown overleaf.

The *Modify Building Options* panel comprises three sub panels, the *Control* one being shown below. The two data boxes on the left can be ignored for the time being. The *Group Symbolic Values* box on the right will, if checked, cause some nodes to be combined, or grouped.

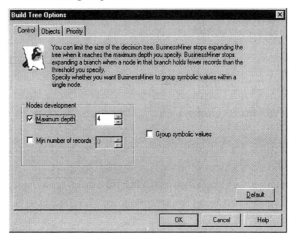

Were this box to have been ticked before creating the dates nodes, the resulting nodes will be as shown below.

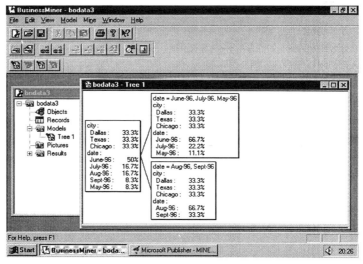

Note that the built-in intelligence of Business Objects has decided on two groups, after taking *discriminating powers* into consideration. These grouping decisions of Business Objects can be overridden by the user by using the *Group* and *Ungroup* options of the *Model* menu. Two or more nodes are grouped by highlighting them (using the *shift* key with the mouse) and activating the *Group* option. A node is ungrouped by highlighting it and activating the *Ungroup* option.

8.2 Expand <u>Selection</u> One Level

Like the *Expand Selection With* option, described above, this option causes Business Objects to create a new set of "child" nodes under a highlighted node. However, rather than inviting the user to choose an object on which to base the new nodes, Business Objects itself selects the object with the highest priority (see p145) or, if no priorities have been assigned by the user, with the highest *discriminating power,* which has not already been used in the path leading up to the node currently highlighted.

The discriminating power of any object in any node will always be known by the Business Objects software and is an indication of the variety of its distinct values (i.e. the number of its distinct values as a proportion of the average number of distinct values of other objects in the same node). Note that the discriminating power of objects will differ from one node to another, simply because there will be different mixes of object values from node to node. Discriminating powers can be viewed in the panel invoked via the *Expand Selection With* option of the *Model* menu. The *Cancel* button should be pressed after viewing the panel; otherwise, the *Expand Selection With* process, described above, will be triggered.

The influence of Discriminating Powers can be overridden by the user through the assignment of *priorities*. These are assigned via the *Priority* sub panel of the *Modify Building Options* option of the *Model* menu, shown overleaf.

All the objects made available for the mining process are listed on the left. Those needing to be assigned priorities can be added to the window on the right via the *Add* button after being highlighted. Priorities can be removed by removing the objects from the right window via the *Remove* button. Objects in the right window can be rearranged vertically via the *Top, Up, Down* and *Bottom* buttons on the right.

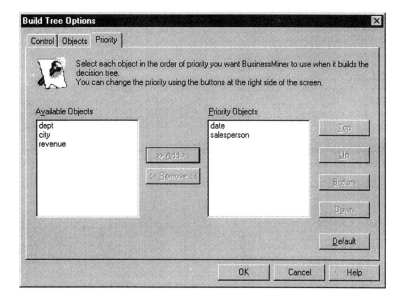

Note that nodes can be removed from the tree through the use of the *Collapse Selection* and *Collapse Tree One Level* options of the *Model* menu. *Collapse Selection* removes all nodes emanating from the highlighted node (children, grandchildren etc). *Collapse Tree One Level* removes the highlighted node plus all other nodes in the same set; plus all other sets emanating from parent nodes within the same set as the parent node of the highlighted node.

8.3 Expand <u>Tree</u> One Level

This option is almost identical to *Expand <u>Selection</u> One Level,* the only difference being that new nodes will be created not only from the node currently highlighted but from all the other nodes which share the same parent node. For example, highlighting the node shown on the left below could trigger the creation of all the new nodes shown on the right.

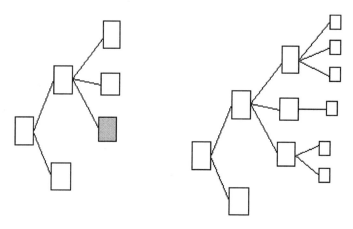

8.4 Expand Selection with Next

Highlighting any node other than an outermost one (for which this option will be unavailable) and selecting this option will remove all child (and grandchildren etc) nodes emanating from the highlighted node and replace them with one set of child nodes based on the next object in the priority (or discriminating power) order to the object on which the removed node set was based. This option is therefore essentially a "go back a step and re-build" option.

8.5 Expand Selection

This option is similar to the *Expand Selection One Level* option except that Business objects continues building new node sets from each new node created, each time using the object with the next highest priority or discriminating power. The tree-building process will stop according to the *stop criteria* specified by the user (or defaulted by Business Objects). Default stop criteria can be changed by the user via the *Control* sub panel of the *Modify Building Options* panel, shown on page 143. Two criteria can be specified:

Maximum depth	The number of nodes in the node chain from root node to outermost node.
Minimum number of records	Nodes that would represent fewer data source records than this minimum value will not be created.

8.6 Mining

Each node represents a distinct subset of the source data and will be associated with a particular set of conditions. For each node, the Business Objects *Data Mining* tool will produce two different kinds of results, depending on whether the node declared as the *output* object is numerical or non numerical.

For numerical output objects:

Minimum, maximum, average and standard deviation, unless the user has specified value ranges (referred to in Business Objects terms as *thresholds*), in which case the results will be the same as for non numerical output objects

For non-numerical output objects:

The number of records associated with each distinct value of the object, together with the proportion they represent of the total number of records represented in the node

For relatively small decision trees, the nodes can be visually examined from the diagram window. For larger trees, it would be useful to get Business Objects to search for them on behalf of the user. This can be achieved in three ways:

Alerters
Discovering rules
What if analyses

8.7 Alerters

Setting alerters is the process of getting Business Objects to assign colors to nodes. This is achieved via the *Alerters* sub panel of the *Modify Display Options* panel, invoked via the *Model* menu. The panel is shown below and is used to assign a particular *color* to a particular *proportion value* range of a particular *distinct value* of a particular *object*.

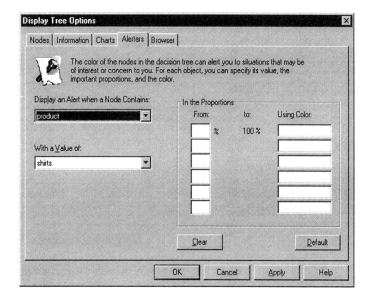

8.8 Discovering Rules

While the *alerters* facility assigns colors to results which fall within user-specified value ranges, the *discovering rules* facility reveals associated record selection criteria (or *rules*) i.e. for a particular *proportion value* range of a particular *distinct value* of a particular object. Users are also able to specify the order in which those conditions are presented. The panel through which these user specifications are declared is shown below and is invoked via the *Discover Rules* option of the *Mine* menu.

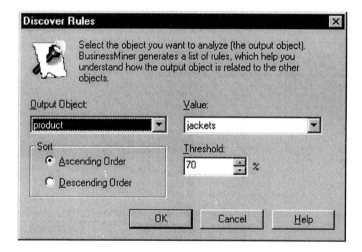

Below is an example of how the record selection criteria is presented.

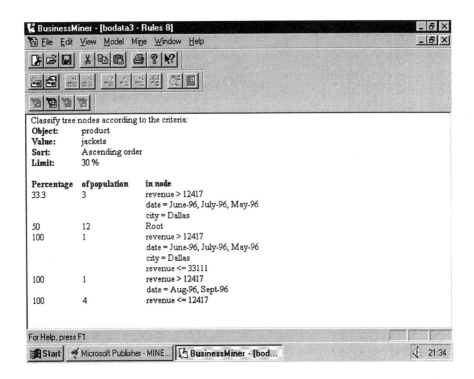

8.9 What If Analysis

The *What If* facility is effectively the reverse of *Discover Rules* in that the user specifies the rules (record selection criteria) and the computer displays the corresponding node results. The *What If* facility is invoked via a *Mine* menu which presents the panel shown below.

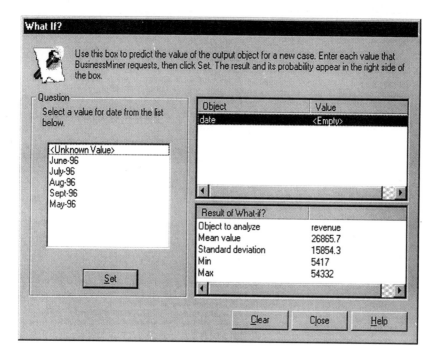

The object on which the first branch of the decision tree is based will be displayed in the top right window. In the left hand window will be either (a) a pick-list of its distinct values (for non numerical objects) or (b) an invitation to enter a value (for numerical objects).

In the bottom right window will be displayed the results of the *What If* analysis, and this will be in terms of the object declared as the *output ob*ject. At this opening stage, these results will refer to the entire (unfiltered) source data and will be either (a) the relative proportions of each distinct value of the *output* object (for non numerical *output* objects) or (b) the minimum, maximum, average and standard deviation (for numeric *output* objects).

On selecting a value from the pick-list (or entering a numerical value) in the left window and activating the *Set* button, the results will be revised accordingly and a new object will appear in the top right hand window. The *What If* analysis is progressed as described above, selecting from the pick-list or entering a numerical value.

At any stage, any of the objects listed in the top right window can be clicked and a new value selected/entered for it. The results will be adjusted accordingly. Alternatively, the whole *What If* process can be restarted by activating the *Clear* button.

CHAPTER 9

User Administration

C hapter 4 describes how Business Objects Designers build *Universes*. Each Universe will be associated with a particular database on a particular server platform. But how are end users able to access the Universes created by Designers, not to mention the server databases which lie behind them? In other words, how are Universes transferred from the designer's PC to end users' PCs? This task is carried out by a third type of Business Objects person: the *Supervisor*.

The Supervisor's responsibility is to "distribute" Universes to users, and this is achieved through the use of a specially reserved area on a server platform (actually a database) referred to in Business Objects terms as the *Repository*. It is to the Repository that designers send their Universes in order to be accessed by users, provided of course that both the designer's and users' PCs can be remotely linked to the Repository's server platform.

Note that the server platform on which the Repository is based has no bearing on the individual server platforms on which the business information databases associated with individual Universes are based. The Repository can reside on one server and individual Universes on others. On the other hand, the Repository and all the Universes to which it refers can reside in the same database on the same server platform.

Note also that documents (reports and associated queries) can also be sent to the Repository to make them publicly accessible, and that both designers and users can send them there.

The Universe and document storage areas of the Repository (or, in Business Objects terms, *domains*) are "protected" by a third area: the *security* domain, and it is by controlling this domain that the Supervisor is able to dictate who is allowed to access what (e.g. who is allowed to create and update Universes in the Repository and who to access a given Universe as end users.

The "who" referred to above is, to the Business Objects software, nothing more than a username and password. By assigning permission for username X to update Universe Y in the Repository, the Supervisor is effectively registering that user as a designer.

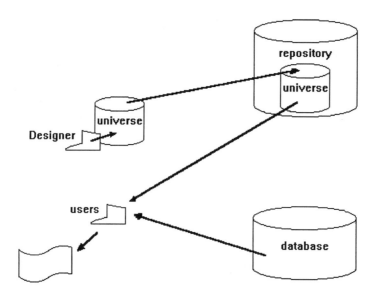

When the Business Objects' Supervisor module is installed on a PC, it will create a special set of (empty) tables in a nominated server database. These constitute a Repository. The Supervisor can then populate the Repository with usernames and passwords, on one hand, and Universes on the other. Access rights can then be established by arranging the two into a matrix.

Note that end users and designers do not need to be aware of the server location of either the Repository or any Universes. The software within users' and designers' PCs *will* of course need to know. In fact, users' and designers' PCs will only need to keep the *Repository's* server (and database) location on their hard disks, since the server locations of individual Universes are known and managed by the Repository. This makes Universe server locations not only secure but "dynamic" in that they can be changed at any time without users and designers knowing anything about it. The server location of the Repository is incidentally held in encoded format so that the task of installing user and designer modules can be delegated to the users and designers themselves without loss of security. That is, the Supervisor can supply users and designers with an encoded file containing the Repository server location at the time software modules are supplied. The Business Objects *Supervisor* software module does the encoding itself, and the Business Objects *Designer* and *User* software modules do the decoding.

A better solution would be to keep one copy of each Business Objects software module, plus the encoded file of Repository location details, in an area of a central server and allow all users read-access to it, perhaps as a virtual drive on their PCs.

On installing Business Objects software modules, end users and designers will need to inform the supervisor of their chosen passwords. The Supervisor can then enter these into the Repository and provide the user with appropriate access rights to Universes.

This is how end users initiate a Business Objects session:

As soon as the Business Objects software module is invoked, the end user will be prompted for a password. The module will then access the repository and, after validating the username and password, will send the user a pick-list of all the Universes he or she has been authorized to access. On selecting one, all the Universe's details (the server location of its database and details of its objects) will be sent across from the Repository into the user's PC, overwriting any details there from previous sessions (thus always providing the user with the latest version). The user can now build and run queries against the Universe's database, and analyze and create reports from the results.

This is how designers will initiate a Business Objects session:

As soon as the Business Objects software module is invoked, the designer will be prompted for a password. The module will then access the repository and validate the username and password. The designer is then free to send across to the Repository the latest version of any Universe he or she has been given permission to maintain, overwriting any previous version already in the Repository. Transferring a Universe version to the Repository effectively places it "into production".

The repository is thus a "central bank" where Universes and documents are held for public use and protected by a "security clearing house" through which end users and designers are given access rights.

The access rights assigned by the supervisor are not restricted to universes but can include software modules (along with a range of qualifications described later). The three types of Business Object user described thus far (supervisor, end user and designer) are in reality somewhat of a simplification and the true nature of a given username really depends on the range of modules to which he or she has been granted access. For example, those whose access rights are limited only to the most basic of reporting tools could be described as "novice" users while those with full query-building and report-creating rights might be described as "expert" users. Designers will usually br granted all these permissions plus the ability to create and update Universes. In fact, the Business Objects product already provides Supervisors with a range of suggested user roles, or *profiles*, each associated with access rights to a particular set of modules. By simply assigning a profile to a username, the Supervisor automatically provides the user with access rights to the corresponding modules.

To make the assigning of access rights easier, the Supervisor is able to arrange users into user groups. Access rights to modules, Universes and documents can be assigned to both users and user groups.

This chapter will describe:

9.1 Creating a Repository
9.2 Arranging Users into user groups
9.3 Assigning Access Rights

9.1 Creating a Repository

The Repository is actually a predesigned set of relational database tables, and the first thing to do is to find a server and create a database instance on it. If acceptable, the server and database instance which hold the end users' business data could be used (i.e. those referenced by Universes).

On being installed, the Business Objects *Supervisor* module will automatically create a set of repository tables on any database instance it is directed to. The supervisor can then start to populate those tables with information about:

- Universes
- Users and user groups
- An access rights matrix of Universes versus users
- An access rights matrix of Business Objects modules versus users

A Repository is automatically created when the Objects Supervisor module is installed. The first screen to appear is shown below and will prompt for username and password. These are always GENERAL and SUPERVISOR, respectively, at this early stage, but will sensibly need to be changed later on.

The welcome screen shown below is accepted via the *Begin* button.

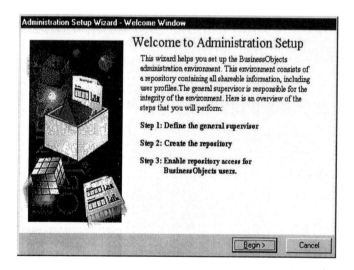

The next screen offers three alternatives. Only the first (Create a default installation) will be described here.

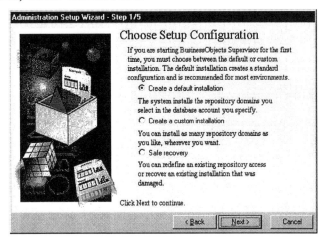

The *Next* button presents the screen below. This screen is used to change the installation supervisor name and password (GENERAL/SUPERVISOR) to a more appropriate one.

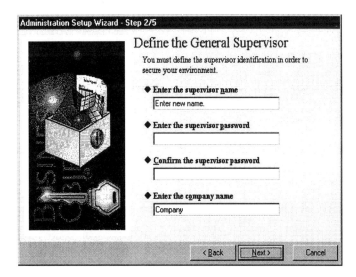

The *Next* button presents the screen shown below, through which a *connection* is declared.

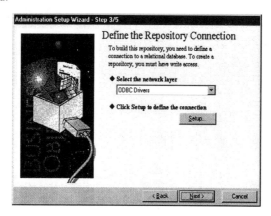

A *connection* is a combination of database instance (for ORACLE) or file (for Microsoft ACCESS), and a driver (SQL*Net for ORACLE and ODBC for MS ACCESS). These are declared via the *Setup* button and it is suggested that advice be sought from your system administrator.

The installation procedure for the Supervisor module is now complete. Whenever the module is invoked, the panel below will prompt for username and password (as declared on the previous page). The OK button will present the main Supervisor screen shown overleaf.

The main Supervisor screen comprises two windows. To the left are users (the Supervisor being the only one established to date). Users can be arranged into groups, and these are shown as folders. The shapes of the icons showing against each user indicate their *role* (the Supervisor's icon being a bunch of keys). Individual users and user groups can be assigned a range of specific access rights.

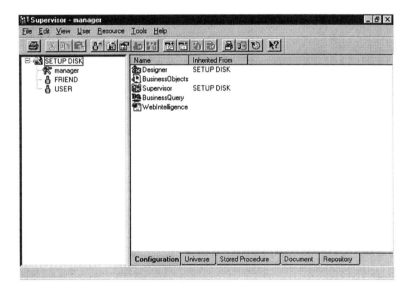

To the right are the *resources* (Business Objects software modules) assigned to the highlighted user on the left. This right panel (the *Configuration* panel) is one of five sub panels.

9.2 Arranging Users into User groups

A user must be a member of at least one group. User groups are created via the *New Group* button (shown right) or menu options *User/New/Group*. A sub group is created by highlighting an existing group in the left window and following the procedure just described for creating a new user group.

A user is assigned to a group by highlighting a group or sub group and either using the *New User* button (shown left) or menu options *User/New/User*. Note that a user can be a member of more than one group or sub group. User groups, sub groups, and users themselves can be assigned properties (or, rather, their default properties can be modified).

Users can be moved or copied between groups by dragging and dropping their icons into the left window or by highlighting the user and pressing the *Add User to Group* button (shown right). This will open up the panel below in which a group and profile (role) are specified.

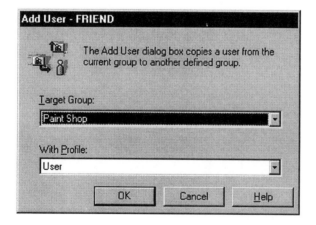

All mention of groups from now on will also apply to sub groups.

The properties of a group can be modified by using the button shown left or alternatively clicking the right mouse button on the group's icon in the left window and selecting *Properties* from the pop-up menu. This will invoke the first of four sub panels (*Definition*), shown below, which simply echos the group name and its parent group (for sub groups). The tick box at the bottom of the panel enables the group to be temporarily disabled (the same effect can be achieved by highlighting a group's icon and using the button shown right).

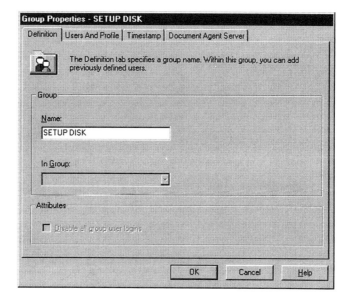

The second sub panel (*Users* and *Profile*) of the *Group Properties* window is shown below, and allows users to be added to groups and assigned profiles there, or removed from groups.

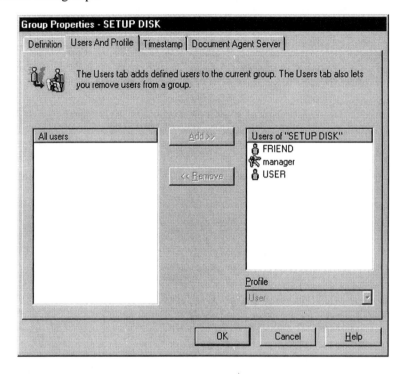

All users are displayed on the left and only those which are members of the group are displayed on the right. Users are added to the group by highlighting them on the left and using the *Add* button. Users are removed from the group by highlighting them on the right and using the *Remove* button.

A user can be assigned a profile by highlighting it in the right side (because the profile is only assigned to the user in association with its membership of a particular group) and setting the profile in the box at the lower right of the screen shown above, via pop-up list.

The third sub panel (*Timestamp*) of the *Group Properties* window is shown below and is used to restrict the accessibility of Business Objects modules by users of a group to particular dates and times.

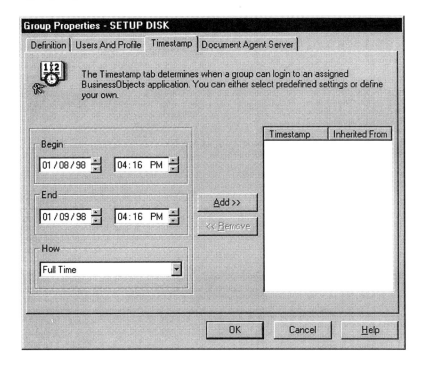

Any number of "timestamps" can be created and these are assembled in the left area of the screen and applied via the *Add* button.

Applied timestamps are displayed in the right area of the screen together with a frequency (the *How* box) specification. An example might be "between September 4th and November 5th on Mondays only between the hours of 9am and 5-30pm".

The fourth sub panel of the *Group Properties* window (*Document Agent Server*) is shown below and allows a *document administrator* to be assigned. There can only be one document administrator in any group. This sub panel enables one of the group's members to be assigned that role. An additional password will need to be established and a Repository (domain) specified. The *Disable Login* check box allows the agent to be temporarily disabled.

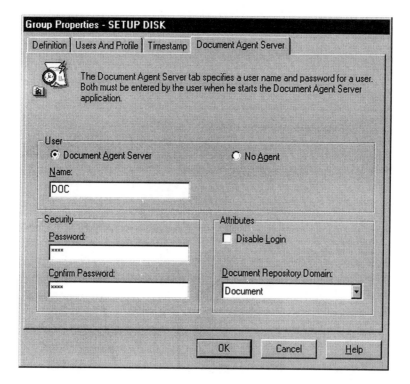

Once these details have been stored in the Repository, only the specified user will be able to invoke the *Document Agent* module. This user will need to enter his or her password every time the module is invoked.

User, as opposed to group, properties can be modified by highlighting a user icon and either activating the *Properties* button (shown left) or using menu options *User/Properties*. Both will invoke the properties panel shown below.

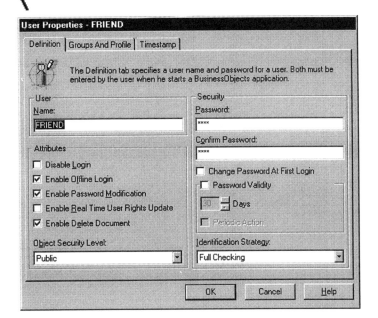

The screen has three sub panels, the first (*Definition*) shown above. Near the top are declared name and password and in the middle left a range of check-box attributes. These allow the user to:

- Be prevented from logging in for the time being
- Be able to log in without accessing the Repository
- Change his or her password
- Automatically receive access-right updates as soon as they are changed (rather than have to wait until the next session is invoked)
- Delete unwanted documents

There are five *Object Security levels* which the Designer can assign to objects of a Universe. These are: *private, confidential, restricted, controlled* and *public.* These are arranged hierarchically, the latter being the default. The supervisor is able to assign the same security level to users. Thus, a user who has, for example, been assigned *restricted* will be able to access all objects of types: *public, controlled* and *restricted.*

The second sub panel (*Groups* and *Profile*) of the *User Properties* screen is shown below and enables users to be assigned to groups.

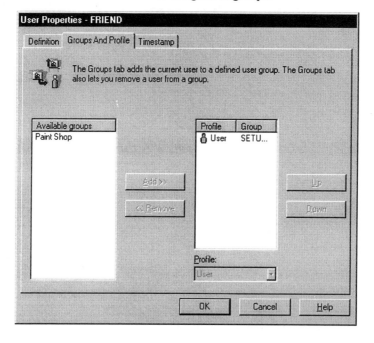

All groups are shown on the left, and those to which the user currently in focus has been assigned are shown on the right. The user is added to one or more groups by highlighting the group(s) on the left and using the *Add* button. The user is removed from one or more groups by highlighting the group(s) on the right and using the *Remove* button.

Once placed into a group, the user can be assigned a profile as a member of that group, via the profile box to the lower right of the screen.

The third sub panel (*Timestamp*) of the *User Properties* screen is shown below and used to restrict the accessibility of Business Objects modules to users to particular dates and times.

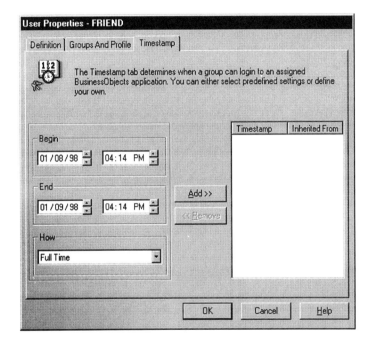

Any number of timestamps can be created and these are assembled in the left area of the screen and applied via the *Add* button.

Applied timestamps are displayed in the right area of the screen together with a frequency (the *How* box) specification. An example might be: "between September 4th and November 5th on Mondays only between the hours of 9am and 5-30pm".

9.3 Assigning Access Rights

This section describes how users and user groups are assigned access rights as a means of controlling accessibility to modules, universes and documents (reports and associated queries).

9.3.1 Modules

In the right window of the main Supervisor screen, shown below, are shown the modules allowed to be used by the user currently highlighted in the left hand window.

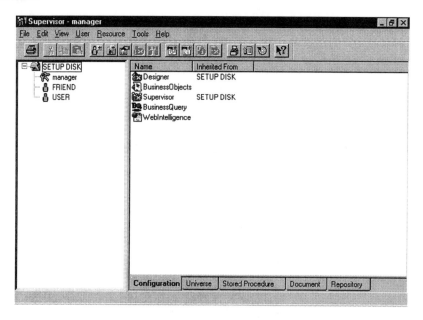

Note that particular sets of modules are assigned automatically to users by default, according to the *profiles* assigned to those users. There are three modules and five profiles, and the default "modules versus profiles matrix" is shown overleaf.

	supervisor module	Designer module	User module
General Supervisor	*	*	*
Supervisor	*		*
Designer		*	*
Supervisor/Designer	*	*	*
End user			*

Note that specific modules can be temporarily disabled (for *all* users) by highlighting them in the right window of the main Supervisor screen (p 163) and using the button shown right.

The modules that have been made accessible to a particular user can be part-restricted on a variety of levels via the *Attributes* dialogue panel (shown below), obtained by double-clicking a user's assigned module in the right window of the main Supervisor screen.

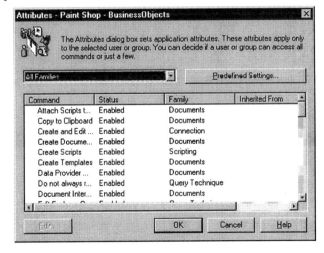

The user and module name are shown at the top of the screen. Listed in the window are all the individual commands associated with the module whose use can be restricted for this particular user. By default all the commands have a status of *enabled.* The status of an individual command can be changed by double-clicking on it to reveal the following pick-list of four status options:

- Disable.
- Disable and also hide from the user all mention of the command.
- Enable
- Inherit the status from an ascendant group (only applicable where the group associated with the selected user is a sub group).

9.3.2 Universes

The second of the sub panels of the main Supervisor screen (*Universe*) allows Universes to be assigned to users and user groups. The sub panel is shown below.

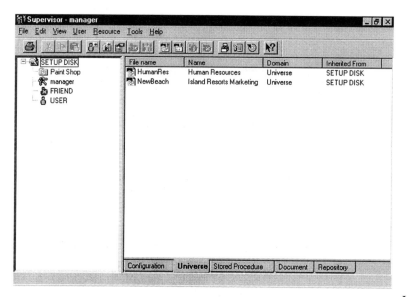

Uni

verses already assigned to users and user groups will be shown in the window. Note that only those Universes that have been *exported* to the Repository by designers will be "known" by the Supervisor module. To assign a Universe to a user, or user group, the user or group is highlighted in the left window of the Main Supervisor screen and either the button shown left used or menu options *Resource/Link/Universe*. This action invokes the *Link Universes* panel in which are listed all the Universes known to the Repository. Highlighting one or more of them and pressing the OK button will close the panel and copy the selected Universes into the panel shown on the previous page.

Having assigned a Universe to a user or user group, further part-restrictions can be applied by double-clicking on the universe in the *Universe* sub panel. This will invoke the *Universe Properties* panel, shown below, which comprises six sub panels. The first (*Definition*) is shown below. Although Universes are actually created by designers, once copied into the Repository, the supervisor is able to give it a description and a "connection" (server and database location).

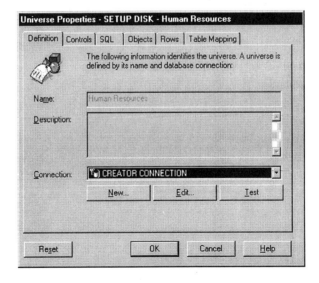

A *Connection* will need to be changed whenever the database referred to by a Universe is physically moved to another server. Such moves will be transparent to end users.

The second sub panel (*Controls*) is shown below and allows restrictions to be applied to the running of database queries. These include:

- Setting a ceiling on the number of rows returned
- Setting a ceiling on execution runtime
- Specifying that a warning message be given when execution time is exceeded
- Setting a ceiling on the amount of text brought back for *long* text objects

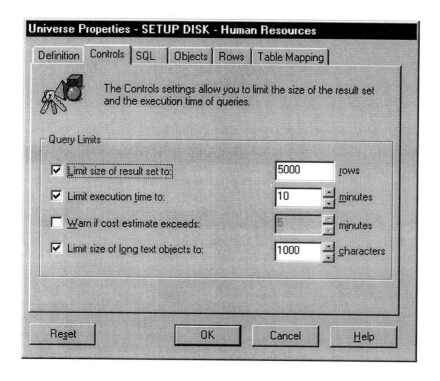

The third sub panel (*SQL*) of the *Universe Properties* panel is shown below and allows the following restrictions to be applied to SQL construction:

- Allow nested sub queries to be created
- Allow the set operators (intersect, union and minus) to be applied
- Enable complex operators to be made available in query panels
- Enable queries involving two or more contexts to be run as separate queries

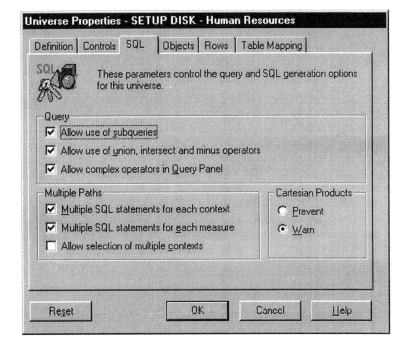

- Allow the execution of queries involving measure objects from different tables
- Allow loops to be involved in queries (when two queries will be run to produce separate results)
- Allow queries involving Cartesian products
- Issue warning messages when Cartesian products are detected

The fourth sub panel (Objects) of the *Universe Properties* panel is shown below and allows specific objects of the Universe to be placed out of bounds.

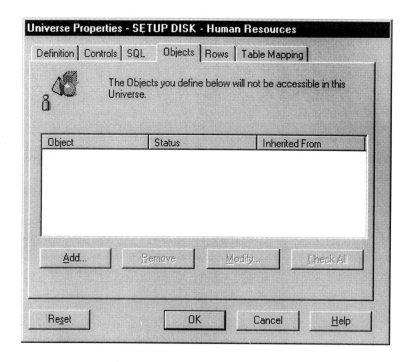

Any objects already placed out of bounds will be shown. The *Add* button is used to add new ones to the list.

The fifth sub panel (*Rows*) of the *Universe Properties* panel allows the supervisor to restrict access to specified rows in a specified database table. The rows are specified by declaring an SQL *where-clause.*

The *Rows* sub panel is shown below and will show any row restrictions already established.

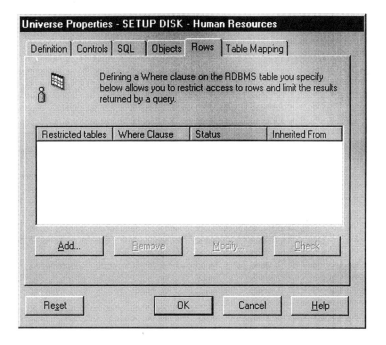

To add a new restriction, the *Add* button is activated to invoke a panel in which a table and where-clause can be specified. If the table name is known it can be keyed in; otherwise, the *Select* button can be used to invoke a pick-list of tables.

The sixth and final sub panel (*Table Mapping*) of the *Universe Properties* panel allows tables referred to by the Universe's objects to be changed. These changes will be transparent to end users and are best understood by imagining that the table names mentioned in the Universe's object definitions are really just synonyms whose underlying tables can be changed here.

The *Table Mapping* sub panel is shown below, in which any mappings already applied will be displayed. The *Add* button is used to add new mappings.

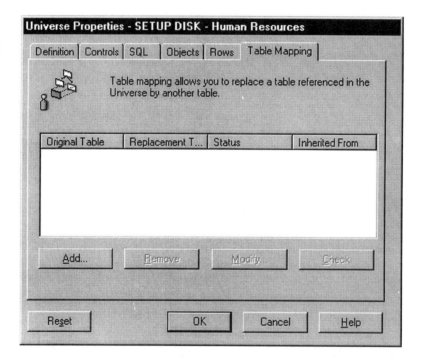

9.3.3 Documents (Reports and Associated Queries)

As well as giving users and user groups access to modules and Universes, they can be given access to documents, that is, reports and associated queries (created by designers and end users) that have been *exported* to the Repository.

The *Document* tab at the bottom of the main Supervisor screen places the *Documents* window into the right side of the screen, as shown below. Using menu options *Resource/Link/Document* has the same effect.

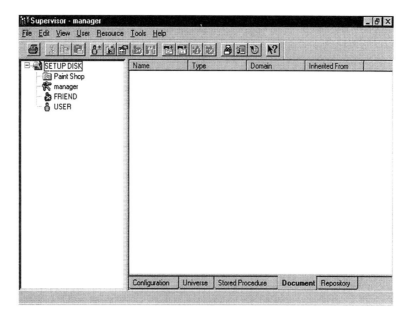

Any documents already assigned will be showing. Highlighting a user or user group in the left window and using the *Add* button will invoke the *Link Documents* panel in which all the Repository's documents and templates are offered for selection.

CHAPTER 10

Business Query

T he Business Objects *Business Query* tool enables database queries to be built, maintained and run from within a Microsoft *Excel* session. Query results will appear in Excel worksheet cells designated by the user.

Section 5.1 describes how database queries are maintained. Query results returned to Excel worksheets are much the same as the report tables described in sections 5.2 and 6.2.

This chapter describes the use of the tool and is structured as follows:

10.1 Introduction

When the Business Query tool is installed it will need to be referenced to Microsoft Excel. This is achieved by invoking Excel and selecting the *Add-Ins* menu option (shown below). If "Business Query 4.0 Add-In" does not appear in the window of the Add-Ins panel (shown overleaf), the *Browse* button is activated and file bqapi.xll selected from the Business Objects folder.

Double-clicking "Business Query 4.0 Add-In" in the window below will cause the
window to close and *BusinessQuery* to appear as a new menu option in Microsoft
Excel's menu bar.

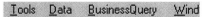

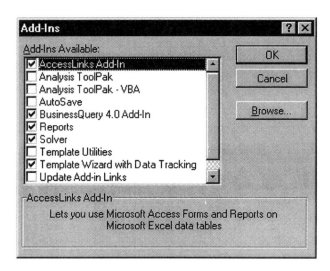

The procedures described above are carried out just once, as part of the
installation process.

Whenever Business Objects queries need to be accessed within a Microsoft
Excel session, the *BusinessQuery* menu option is selected and the *Load* option
double-clicked from the pop-up menu.

On loading the Business Objects software, the following panel will prompt
for username and password, unless
default ones have been specified, as
described in Section 10.4.

If during the current Excel session, the user wishes to login to Business Objects under another username, the *Login-As* option of the *BusinessQuery* menu is selected to redisplay the panel above. The *AutoLoad* option of the *BusinessQuery* menu will cause the Business Objects software to be loaded automatically whenever Excel itself is invoked. The *Unload* option of the *BusinessQuery* menu will quit the Business Objects software and clear it out of memory.

The OK button will close the panel above and bring the Business Objects  toolbar onto the Excel screen, as shown left. The toolbar buttons provide the following functionality, from left to right:

- Allows a new Business Objects query to be created.
- Inserts the data retrieved by an existing Business Objects query into the Excel worksheet without rerunning the query, the first column of the first row of the query results being inserted into the currently highlighted Excel worksheet cell.
- Allows an existing Business Objects query to be modified.
- Allows an existing Business Objects query to be rerun (i.e. its results to be *refreshed* in the Excel worksheet).
- Allows *all* existing Business Objects queries to be rerun (i.e. all their results to be refreshed in the Excel worksheet).
- Allows existing queries to be managed (as described in Section 10.3).
- Allows *all* existing Business Objects queries to be rerun (and all results thereby refreshed) but in the order in which the queries are listed by the query manager (described on page 193).
- View/modify query options (of the query currently in focus).
- Online help.

Most of these actions are available from the BusinessQuery menu.

10.2 Building and Running Queries

The processes of creating, modifying and running database queries are described in Section 5.1. For these activities to be made possible, users need access to Business Objects Universes held on remote servers. Ordinary Business Objects users, as opposed to Microsoft Excel users with access to Business Objects software, will automatically be provided with downloaded Universe information whenever they invoke their Business Objects software. Microsoft Excel users, on the other hand, will need to initiate the downloading of Universe information themselves. They will do it once to obtain Universe information in the first place and then retrigger the download whenever they get word that the Universe has been updated.

Downloading Universe information is invoked via the *Universes* option of the *BusinessQuery* menu, which will open up the panel shown below right. A Universe is highlighted from the list of those available. Note that if the remote server version of the Universe has been updated since it was last downloaded, "To Be Refreshed" will appear in the Universe's status field. The *Import* button triggers the downloading. The *Refresh* button merely refreshes the list of Universes in the window. The *List of Values* button refreshes all the locally held Lists of Values associated with the highlighted Universe (Lists of Values are explained on pages 42, 47 and 62).

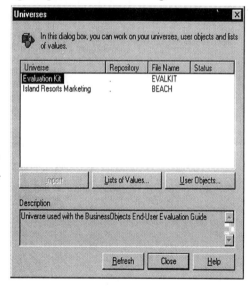

The toolbar button shown below right will open up the *New Query* panel below it from which a Universe can be selected and in which a new query can be named and described.

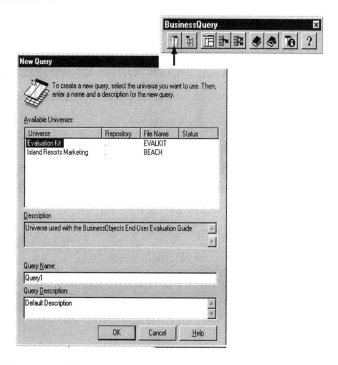

The OK button will invoke the *Query Builder* screen, which is shown on page 58. Query building is fully described in Section 5.1.

When the query is run (via the *Run* button in the *Query Builder* screen), its results will be refreshed and (re)inserted into the Excel worksheet. For new queries, the first column of the first row of the query results will be inserted into the currently highlighted Excel worksheet cell. Note that the query definition and its results (from when the query was last run) will be stored in a file with extension .bqy in the *userbqy* folder of the Business Objects folder of the PC's hard disk.

The tool button shown right is used to insert the results of an existing query into the Excel worksheet without rerunning the query, the first column of the first row of the query results being inserted into the currently highlighted Excel worksheet cell.

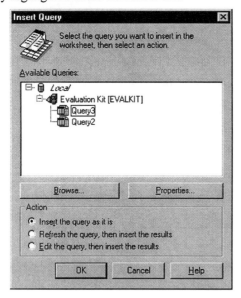

A query can be selected from the list of queries stored locally on the PC's hard disk in the *userbqy* folder of the Business Objects folder. The *Browse* button can be used to access queries stored elsewhere. At the bottom of the panel are three action check boxes. These have the following effects:

- Causes the current results of the selected query (i.e. those obtained when the query was last run) to be inserted into the highlighted Excel worksheet cell without rerunning the query.

- Causes the query to be rerun first (i.e. *refreshing* the results) before the results are inserted into the worksheet.

- Opens up the *QueryBuilder* screen (see page 58).

Queries highlighted in the list can be deleted, duplicated and renamed by clicking the right mouse button and selecting *Delete*, *Duplicate* and *Rename* respectively from the pop-up menu.

The *Properties* button opens up the *Query Properties* panel below in which the following information about the query is displayed:

- Universe
- Name and description (the latter is updatable)
- The creator's name and the date and time the query was created
- The date and time the query was last rerun

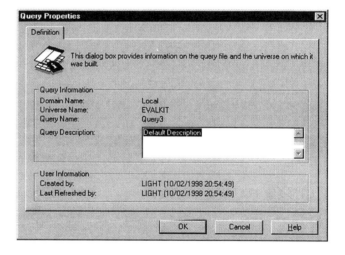

The *Query Properties* panel can also be opened up via the toolbar button shown here.

Existing queries can be modified via the *Edit Query* button shown right, which will open up the *Query Builder* panel shown on page 58. Refer to Section 5.1 for details about editing queries. An alternative to using this button is the *Edit Query* option of the *BusinessQuery* menu.

The results from an existing query can be refreshed in the Excel worksheet (i.e. the query rerun) by highlighting any cell containing the results of the query and

using the *Refresh Query* button, shown left. An alternative to using this button is the *Refresh Query* option of the *BusinessQuery* menu.

The button shown right is used to refresh the results of *all* the queries contained in the Excel worksheet, and in the order specified (see page 193). An alternative to using this button is the *Refresh All Queries* option of the *BusinessQuery* menu.

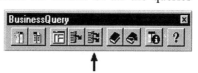

The overall management of the queries in the Excel worksheet (described in the following section) is achieved through the *Query Director* screen, shown overleaf, which is opened up via the button shown left (provided at least one query

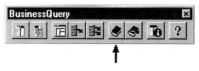

exists in the Excel worksheet. An alternative to using this button is the *QueryDirector* option of the *BusinessQuery* menu.

10.3 Managing Queries

The Query Director screen, shown below, enables all queries contained within the Excel worksheet to be easily identified and centrally controlled. The panel comprises three sub   panels, or tabs.

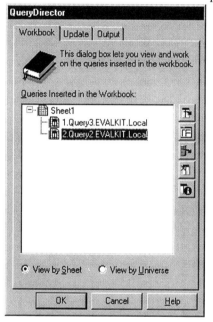

The first (*Workbook*) tab lists all the queries within the Excel worksheet. These can be displayed by worksheet or Universe, according to which radio button is checked at the bottom of the screen. In the *worksheet* view (shown above), the information provided includes a number indicating the order in which the queries are triggered (when *Refresh All Queries* is selected) and query name, universe name and either "local" or Repository name (Repositories are described in Chapter 9). For example, in the panel above, the first query to be triggered is *Query3* which is associated with Universe EVALKIT. If one of the queries listed is clicked, the cells of the Excel worksheet to which the query's results are directed are highlighted.

Note that five buttons are available, arranged vertically down the right side of the panel. These, from top to bottom, provide the following functionality, which is directed toward the query currently highlighted in the window:

- Inserts the results of the query into the worksheet without rerunning the query (i.e. without refreshing the query's results). This would be appropriate where a query file (containing both query and results) has been sent to the user's PC by another user (transferring query files is discussed on page 194) and does not need to be rerun.

- Allows the query to be edited by opening up the Query Builder screen (described on page 58).

- Reruns the query, thereby refreshing its results in the worksheet.

- Removes the query from the worksheet, with the option of keeping its results in the worksheet (and making them static).

- Examines the query's properties (see page 189).

Note that any of the queries listed can be renamed by clicking on its name twice (but not double-clicking it) and keying in a new name.

The second tab of the Query Director panel (*Update*) is shown overleaf and allows users to change the order in which queries are triggered, when the *Refresh All Queries* action is selected, and to specify their behavior (or *action*) from a choice of three options.

The ordering is changed by highlighting a query and using the up and down buttons on the right side of the panel.

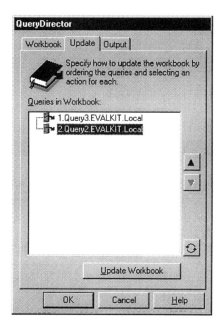

A query's behavior is specified by repeatedly pressing the button with the circular design at the lower right of the panel.

The three behavior, or *action*, options are:

- Reruns the query and inserts its results into the worksheet.
- Inserts the query's current results into the worksheet without rerunning the query
- Effectively disables the query.

The big *Update Workbook* button at the bottom of the panel will rerun *all* the queries (and thereby refresh all their results in the worksheet) in the specified order.

Chapter 9 describes how several endusers are given access to their informational databases through the establishment of a Repository (itself a database) on a central server. Any user whose PC is networked to the Repository is able to query databases. The Repository can hold not only details about databases, but query definitions as well. If a user creates a query and wishes to make it available to other users, he or she can send the query to the Repository.

Queries are sent to, and retrieved from, the central Repository via BusinessQuery menu options *Send To>Users* (or *Send To>Repository*) and *Retrieve from Users*.

When sending queries, they can be either sent "privately" to a named user (or users) or delivered into the hands of the Business Objects supervisor, who can make the queries available to any users or user groups. In either case, the query is sent to the Repository. In the former (user-targeted) case, as soon as all the named users have retrieved queries that have been sent to them from the Repository, the queries will be automatically removed from the Repository.

10.4 General Options

This section describes how the *Business Query* tool can be customized. Selecting *Options* from the *BusinessQuery* menu will open up the screen below.

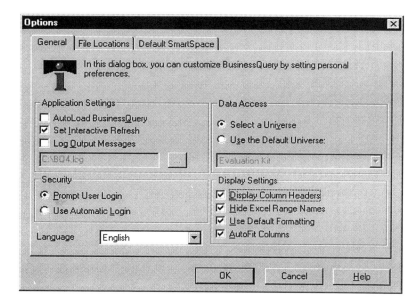

The screen has three sub panels, or tabs, and the leftmost (*General*) is shown above. The check boxes are described as follows:

Application Settings

Autoload Business Query   This causes the Business Query software to be loaded automatically as soon as Microsoft Excel is invoked using the username and password entered for the current session.

Set Interactive Refresh	Deactivating this option will disallow users from creating and editing queries and from updating the Excel worksheet, effectively only allowing queries to be rerun and their results refreshed in the worksheet.
Log Output Messages	Causes all messages to be saved in a file location defaulted to c:\bq4.log, but which location can be changed in the data entry box below the checkbox.

Security

Prompt User Login	When checked, this will ensure that a username and password will be prompted for every time BusinessQuery is loaded.
Use Automatic Login	This is the reverse of the above in that if checked, the Business Query software will not prompt the user for username and password when next launched, but use those entered for the current session instead.

Data Access

Select a Universe	Allows the user to select a Universe.
Use the Default Universe	Will allow the current session user to change the default Universe.

Display Settings

Display Column Headings	Displays/hides column headings in query results inserted into the worksheet.
Hide Excel Range Names	If checked, prevents query names from appearing in the Name Box at the left end of the Excel worksheet's formula bar.

Use Default Formatting   Applies default Business Query formatting (colors) of query results inserted into worksheets.

Autofit Columns   Causes worksheet columns to be automatically resized when necessary to accommodate inserted query results.

Note that the *Display Headings* above can also be applied to individual queries, as explained on page 202.

The second tab (*File Locations*) of the Options screen is shown below and allows file locations for Documents, Universes and Queries to be changed. The window shows the current settings. The *Browse* button is used to change them.

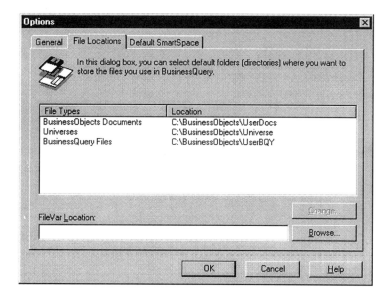

The third tab (*Default SmartSpace*) of the Options screen is shown below and is concerned with the way query results are refreshed in Excel worksheets when a query has been changed to produce more or fewer rows and/or columns. The *SmartSpace* facility enables different *strategies* to be adopted for such eventualities.

The screen is shown below and is essentially divided into three vertical sections.

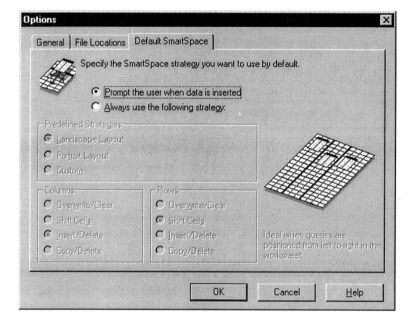

If the top check box of the two located in the uppermost section of the screen is checked, the second and third sections of the screen will be disabled, as shown above. This setting will cause Business Query to halt, just before inserting query results that will impinge on already populated cells in the worksheet, and prompt the user to specify a strategy.

Ticking the second check-box at the top of the screen will enable one of the three default strategies, presented in three check-boxes in the central section of the screen, to be specified. The strategy selected will be automatically applied from then on. A graphical representation of the strategy selected will appear automatically to the right of the screen.

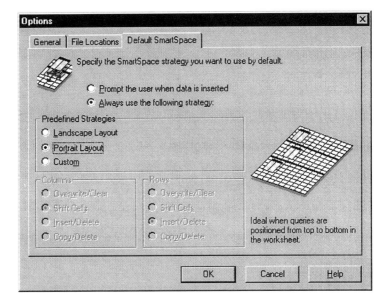

The three options have the following effect:

Landscape Layout

This option should be selected when two or more query results sets are arranged horizontally adjacent to one another in the Excel worksheet. If an existing query has been modified to produce more result columns than before, new worksheet columns will be inserted into the worksheet, thus preserving and shifting to the right all worksheet cells populated from other sources which are positioned to the right of the query results. If fewer result columns are produced, unused worksheet columns are deleted from the worksheet - thereby shifting to the left all the worksheet cells populated from other sources which are positioned to the right of the query results.

The former result rows will be shifted up or down as new rows are added or former ones removed.

Portrait Layout

This option should be selected when two or more query results sets are arranged vertically adjacent to one another in the Excel worksheet. If an existing query has been modified to produce more result rows than before, new worksheet rows will be inserted into the worksheet, thus preserving and shifting downward all worksheet cells populated from other sources which are positioned below the query results. If fewer result columns are produced, unused worksheet rows are deleted from the worksheet, thereby shifting upward all the worksheet cells populated from other sources which are positioned below the query results.

The former columns will be shifted to left or right as new ones are added or former ones removed.

Custom

This option allows users to define their own strategies using the options in the lower part of the screen, shown overleaf, for columns and rows. These are as follows:

Overwrite/Clear

New results simply overwrite old ones. A column whose position in the query's *select statement* has been modified will thus move from its former worksheet column to another.

Shift Cells

Worksheet cells holding the old results are shifted left, right, up or down, as necessary, to accommodate the new query results.

Insert/Delete

Worksheet cells are created or deleted to accommodate the new query results. Neighboring worksheet cells are thus preserved by being shifted out of the way.

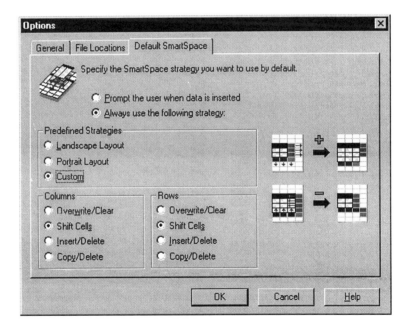

The strategy specified above will become the default for all queries. Note, however, that individual queries can be given their own strategies which can be different from the default. This is achieved as follows:

- The *QueryDirector* toolbar button is activated.

- The query of interest is clicked in the *Workbook* tab of the *Query Director* window (shown on page 191) and the *Properties* button clicked (the bottom button of those vertically arranged on the right).

- The *View in Sheet* tab, shown below, is selected. This displays the current status settings and, at bottom right, the Display Settings described on page 195.

- The *Change* button is clicked and will present the *SmartSpace* window, and define the strategy as described on pages 198 through to the top of this page.

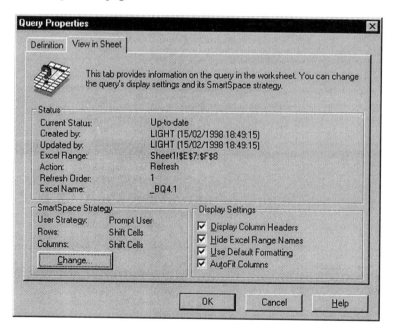

To summarize: Chapter 10 has described how the Business Objects' BusinessQuery software product provides Microsoft Excel users with direct and integral accessibility to remote informational databases.

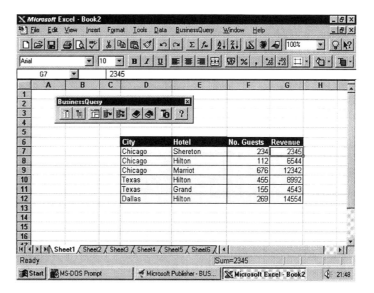

Index

Back | Forward | Home | Reload | Images | Open | Print | Find | Stop

http://www.phptr.com/

What's New? | What's Cool? | Destinations | Net Search | People | Software

PRENTICE HALL

Professional Technical Reference
Tomorrow's Solutions for Today's Professionals.

Keep Up-to-Date with
PH PTR Online!

We strive to stay on the cutting-edge of what's happening in professional computer science and engineering. Here's a bit of what you'll find when you stop by **www.phptr.com**:

Special interest areas offering our latest books, book series, software, features of the month, related links and other useful information to help you get the job done.

Deals, deals, deals! Come to our promotions section for the latest bargains offered to you exclusively from our retailers.

Need to find a bookstore? Chances are, there's a bookseller near you that carries a broad selection of PTR titles. Locate a Magnet bookstore near you at www.phptr.com.

What's New at PH PTR? We don't just publish books for the professional community, we're a part of it. Check out our convention schedule, join an author chat, get the latest reviews and press releases on topics of interest to you.

Subscribe Today! **Join PH PTR's monthly email newsletter!**

Want to be kept up-to-date on your area of interest? Choose a targeted category on our website, and we'll keep you informed of the latest PH PTR products, author events, reviews and conferences in your interest area.

Visit our mailroom to subscribe today! **http://www.phptr.com/mail_lists**